CHRIST ON THE JEWISH ROAD

CHRIST
ON THE JEWISH ROAD

Richard Wurmbrand

HODDER AND STOUGHTON
LONDON SYDNEY AUCKLAND TORONTO

To the memory of
Isac Feinstein and others who gave their lives under the
Nazis and Communists for being
Jews and Christians

CONTENTS

PREFACE

LOOKING BACK ON my life, I, too, am astonished how much I have been through.

For a Christian, life is not retrospective: he wastes no time writing obituaries about what is past; instead, he writes, in the hearts of men, with the pen of the Holy Spirit, the preface to a bright and eternal future. As a rule, memoirs are written by people who no longer have a satisfactory, rich present.

But I have a different reason for recording my memories.

A quarter of a century has passed since I started the work of preaching the Christian message to Jews under particularly difficult circumstances—Fascist terror, war, and later on the Communist regime in Rumania. I have endured the heat of battle in a most important part of the battlefield, where the eternal struggle between light and darkness is waged.

"Thou hast chosen us from amongst the peoples," the Jews declare daily in their synagogues. "Salvation is of the Jews," said Jesus (John 4.22). "The dirty Jews are the cause of all our troubles," say the anti-Semites. The "international" Jew has been copiously depicted in literature.

Some people find in Christianity their true happiness: others hate Christianity and would like to see it destroyed. It is a Jew, Jesus, who is the cause of their happiness or their fury.

Some people benefit from capitalism; others feel they are exploited by the capitalist system, and would like to see it overthrown. No one would deny that the Jews were instrumental at an early point in time in founding this system, and that they still play a highly important role in economic and financial life, out of all proportion to their numbers. Whether you feel attracted or repelled by capitalism, your attitude will to a large extent be determined by Jews, whom you will probably never have seen face to face, as the people who have the final say in the capitalist world are almost always anonymous.

Communism may be to you a source of joy or suffering; it derives from the Jew Marx and a host of Jewish champions of this idea, without whom the revolution in the East would have been impossible. The fate of a farmer in Vietnam, who has never seen a Jew in his life, will, in the last resort, depend on whether he reads the book about the Jew Jesus or the book about the Jew Marx. Whichever triumphs, either the Christian civilisation or the Marxist world, both are closely bound up with a Jewish name.

Some people place their confidence in modern science, whose peak achievement is in atomic physics, a science capable of enabling mankind to live in a Utopia. Others wait, in fear and terror, for the destructive atomic war which they believe will be the final result of this science. In both the West and the East, atomic science is to a large extent in the hands of Jews. Einstein gave the United States a start in atomic weapons. The Jew Teller is the father of the nuclear bomb. The Rosenbergs, Jews, gave atomic secrets to Russia. In scientific books the universe is named after a Jew: we speak of Einstein's universe, as though we lived in this universe as the guests of a Jew.

And this is really so, for we are in very fact the guests of a Jew; only his name is not Einstein, but Jesus Christ. He is a human being and a Jew, but also God—a marvellous God, of whom we read in His holy book, in Paul's Epistle to the Romans: ". . . of whom [the Jews] as concerning the flesh Christ came, who is over all, God blessed for ever" (Rom. 9.5). A people from whom God came!

Mine has not been ordinary missionary work; I have worked among those people who in the holy book of the Christians are called "a chosen people", a people from whom a God has come, but who nevertheless are ignorant of this God, a nation which is either blessed or cursed by millions of people—as the source of their happiness or their misery—a race whose fate has determined and will determine, more than any other nation, the fate of the entire world.

The Jewish people have given to the world the Bible, consisting of the Old and New Testaments, a book written by Jews, but which is at the same time the Word of God—the only book capable of satisfying the spiritual needs of the world. And it will satisfy these needs when it is once again in the hands of those who have written it, and when they gather round Him who is the chief subject of the book, Jesus, the Messiah of the Jews and the Saviour of nations.

The overwhelming majority of mankind lives in dire sin, bereft of the true faith. Murder, exploitation, oppression, fornication, defeat, envy, debauchery and slander are widespread. Mankind is bound to suffer speedy destruction unless it is converted and rouses itself from the spiritual death in which it now lies. But the Scriptures tell us that the conversion of Israel will be life from the dead (Rom. 11.15).

Jesus and the Jews are indissolubly linked to one another. "Where is He that is born King of the Jews?" the Magi enquired when He came into this world (Matt. 2.2). "This is Jesus, the King of the Jews", was the inscription on the Cross (Matt. 27.37).

The Old Testament prophecies have the same message. Moses told the Jews: "The Lord thy God will raise up unto thee a Prophet from the midst of thee, *of thy brethren*" (Deut. 18.15). Isaiah, who prophesied the birth of Jesus eight hundred years before it took place, declared: "Unto *us* a child is born, unto *us* a son is given" (Isa. 9.6)—"us" meaning the Jews. When he foretold the new covenant which Jesus would establish by shedding His blood on the Cross, Jeremiah declared: "Behold . . . I will make a new covenant with the *house of Israel*, and with the *house of Judah*" (Jer. 31.31).

Jesus himself said: "I am not sent but unto the lost sheep of the house of Israel" (Matt. 15.24). He also declared that he was the Saviour of the world, but in the passage above and in similar statements he established his special relationship with the Jewish people.

The intention of my entire missionary work, of which I

give an account in this book, was to make Israel conscious of this relationship, a relationship which can never be broken, however much we may oppose it. The Jew today is no longer what he was two thousand years ago; he is not even the Jew who lived in the ghettos of medieval Europe, from which the French Revolution liberated us. We have made progress in science, art, literature, and in social life: only in religion there is stagnation, or, at least, the progress is not so rapid as in other spheres.

Those Jews may perhaps have had good commonsense reasons for rejecting a carpenter who declared that He was the Saviour of the world. But we are in a much better position than they were to realise who Jesus was. Had He been an ordinary child born outside the bonds of matrimony, an enthusiastic dilettante—as some people believed He was—He would not have conquered as indeed He did.

People of brilliant intellectual powers have paid homage to Him.

The Jew Spinoza declared: "Jesus is the highest symbol of Jewish wisdom."

Rousseau wrote: "If the death of Socrates was the death of a sage, then the death of Jesus was the death of a God."

Strauss, who wrote several works in order to prove that Jesus is not God, nevertheless declares that He is the highest goal to which we can aspire in our thoughts.

Ernest Renan, who caused a great many people to doubt the divinity of Jesus, says that His beauty is eternal and that His kingdom will never come to an end.

Some find it difficult to believe what His disciples said of Him, but let us at any rate believe His enemies, such as the Pharisees who declared: "Master, we know that thou art true, and carest for no man: for thou regardest not the person of men, but teachest the way of God in truth" (Mark 12.14). Judas confessed: "I have betrayed innocent blood." (Matt. 27.4). Pilate said: "I am innocent of the blood of this just person" (Matt. 27.24). The captain of the guard, in charge of the crucifixion, declared: "Truly this was the Son of God." (Matt. 27.54).

Belief in Jesus gives the believer confidence. True belief in

Jesus turns stubborn minds into hearts burning with love. True belief of Jesus breaks down barriers between races and nations.

The Court of the Gentiles in the Temple of Jerusalem was separated from the Holy of Holies by a fence, on which was written in three languages: "He who is not a Jew and passes further will be punished by death". The Christian religion breaks down national boundaries, and makes God's house a place where all peoples meet in prayer.

But someone will raise the objection: If belief in Jesus transforms us into love, how are we to explain the violent conflicts that take place within a Christian congregation, and the disputes between the various confessions? And if Christianity makes the people of every nation brothers, how are we to explain the murderous wars that are waged between Christian nations? Do not the naked facts refute the claims of Christianity?

The answer is that we are still living in prehistoric times, as far as the Christian Church is concerned. The various confessions are merely parts of the framework of the proud and magnificent building which will one day arise.

The task to which those Jews are called who have been converted to belief in Jesus, is to give the world life out of spiritual death. The Scriptures declare that the purpose of saving the Gentiles—who have given what they could—was to make the Jews jealous for their God. The Jews have been called, and specially equipped by God, to give a real inner meaning to the Christian Church. Don't look at the church as she is, but as she will be when the Jews whom she expects will have become Christians, and will give her an unequalled beauty. Then she will be one and burning with love.

God has called me to bring Jews to Christ. When He calls, He always gives a man the capacity and the facilities to obey His call. Every human being possesses spiritual powers of which he himself is ignorant. When he pledges himself in love to Jesus, he discovers what powers are latent within him. Even I, at the beginning of my Christian life, had no idea for how many works I would be used.

For these were not *my* acts: the Christian believer is like a child who is allowed by the driver to hold the steering-wheel of a car, while the driver himself keeps his hands over the child's. The child is delighted to be driving a car—without being able to make a single mistake—because there is someone who is in charge, and knows everything. Even while we are carrying our burdens, we ourselves are borne aloft on eagles' wings.

He who works through His children is the same God who scattered the stars in the firmament of heaven. Within us we have His power enabling us to sacrifice ourselves, that same power which was in the Son when He was crucified for our sakes. Through us the sanctifying power of the Spirit is at work. In us it moves like a mighty storm, and through us this storm arouses others to passionate zeal, because God dwells within us. It is as though the fulness of His grace all but shatters the vessel which is too narrow for Him.

When I look back on these past years, I can seldom discover any logic between what happened and the attitude I adopted at the time. "The heart has its reasons, which reason does not know." The birth of a man's deepest conviction is not the result of a process of thought; the subconscious cannot be trained, and does not behave in a logical way. It does not think in conformity with the ordinary laws of reason. It is in some dreams that one can see the magnitude of man's hidden values. This subconsciousness is the darkness where God likes to dwell: here He has openly done things through me that even I cannot understand. Beyond the world of phenomena perceived through the senses, lies the real, invisible world, the essential world. This is where the divine works; and what is seen in our nature is governed from it.

I do not understand everything that has happened to me, but I believe that my whole life, and the life of all His children, has been planned by God, down to the smallest detail. Our lives are planned in eternity; our lives serve God's purpose. I can be confident, even when I understand nothing.

When I first became a follower of Jesus, I did not want to have quarrels with anyone, I merely wanted to rest from all that had gone before. Religion must put an end to striving, it must bring calm. But a calm life, lived only in love and in the interpretation of the truth, raises new storms; one's religion is attacked, one must defend it, and so, without having wished it, one is at war again. We have to actively put into practice faith and love, and only God knows why, as sons of peace, we do not bring peace, but a sword.

I have come into conflict with many of the Jewish people of whom I am a part. Jews often call Christian Jews traitors to their people. I shall not dwell on this terrible term. It could be said more simply, and with greater love, that the Christian Jews use a different scale of values.

But is it really one's own people who constitute the supreme value? Both the Old and the New Testaments depict as holy a priestess of a Canaanite temple, where religious prostitution was practised. Her name was Rahab. At a point of time when the Jews were going to war, with a view to the complete destruction of the Canaanites, Rahab concluded a pact with the Jews, against the interests of her own people. Was she a traitor? Was she thereby degraded? No, she was a woman who put the new religion—represented by the Jews—above the interests of the people to whom she belonged. In this way she became one of the ancestors of Jesus. She is also honoured by the Mosaic Jews.

We love our people whole-heartedly: but we consider the glory of Christ of more value than our own people. And, faced with the alternative of choosing between Jesus and our people, if they demand that we should renounce Him, we choose Jesus because we know fully that those who do not in truth serve Him, cannot serve their own people best.

When my wife and I became Christians, we found beloved brothers and sisters in all confessions; but no single one of these confessions constitutes the Christian Church. None of them possesses the unadulterated truth, nor a truly burning love. Many Christian pastors are not what a pastor should be; a person in whom Christ is present, an ardent soul who sees the truth, declares it, and carries it out, a man through whom God himself speaks. The sheep are not listened to. The gifts of grace possessed by members of the Church are not sufficiently utilised. They stand unemployed in the marketplace, or else their strength and their ability are not given full scope. The work of the Church lacks the co-ordinated action in which all God's children should take part.

We are the most poorly organised army. Jesus's melancholy remark, that the children of this world are wiser than the sons of light (Luke 16.8) has not inspired us to change things. In the old days a Christian army was recruited in order to win an empty tomb. Why do we not organise an army to win living souls?

When we, who were new to the Christian faith, raised these problems, Christian leaders became angry with us.

There is a club for dwarfs. Membership is open only to persons who are not more than four feet tall. Dwarfs say that they are closest to human perfection, because the first men were taller than those of today; hand in hand with progress, the human form has become smaller. We could in fact set up a club for Christian dwarfs, with a great many members. It is the dwarfs of Christianity who are regarded as the standard, while the giants are considered to be fanatics. The dwarfs, the cold and indifferent, are considered the ones who are wise. I find myself in opposition to people who think along these lines.

Even more, I was opposed to the atheist world. The bodies and souls of many Hebrew Christians bear the scars of wounds received in this struggle. But only the soldier who risks his life is a true soldier, and scars are a soldier's badge of honour.

For twenty-five years I have had one single task, because I knew that it is only the man who concentrates on one goal who can accomplish great things. Amateurs do not make great athletes; nor are those clergymen the best pastors who, apart from being clergymen, are also devoted philatelists, football players, chess players, musicians, politicians, and a great many other things. You may have many gifts, but they must be all subject to the same aim.

I have done only one thing. I have worked for Christ. I am not satisfied with what I have accomplished. If I were, I should not be able to make any progress. But I know that Jesus will forgive me if I have erred in my thought and sinned in my life. He has not abandoned me, and He will help me to do better in future.

And because this is not the work of an individual—the true Christian belongs to the assembly of God's children—I have written this book, in order that what has been right and what has been wrong in what I have accomplished, may serve as a lesson to the Church and to the Jewish people, in order that others may do better.

I SET OUT ON THE ROAD

A German carpenter shows a Jew the way to Christ

It was 1937. Hitler was in power.

In a small village in Rumania, a German carpenter was spending the remaining years of his old age. His name was Christian Wölfkes.

During a revivalist campaign in the Evangelical Lutheran Church, conducted by Pastor Scherg, he had been converted to Christianity. Later on, he joined a congregation of brethren who called themselves "Christians according to the Gospel".

Wölfkes realised that a Christian who is not a missionary, even if on a very small scale, is not fulfilling his duty, which is to be a light for the world. One night when he was seriously ill, a Christian Jew watched by his bedside. In gratitude, from the depths of his heart, he now longed to be used to bring Jews to Christ.

His daily prayer was: "O Lord, I have served Thee on earth, and on earth I desire my reward. I pray that I may not die before I have converted a Jew to the faith. But there are no Jews in this neighbourhood, and I am old, sick and poor. I am not able to go and look for them elsewhere. Thou art all-powerful. Bring a Jew here to me in my village, and I promise I will do my utmost to convert him to the faith."

The first Jew who came to the village that spring was myself. I do not know if there was ever a girl so passionately wooed by her lover as I was wooed by this old man, who saw in me the answer to his prayer.

He gave me the Bible to read.

I had read it before, but it had not made any impression on

me. But the Bible I now held in my hand was not like any other Bible: later I discovered its secret. Wölfkes and his wife were spending many hours daily praying for the conversion of myself and my wife. Actually, I couldn't really read it; rather, I wept over it. My tears always started to flow whenever I compared my selfish and wretched life with the life of Him who went around doing good.

Wölfkes allowed the Bible and his own prayer to work in my heart. He hardly talked to me at all. Instinctively he knew, what so many trained missionaries do not know, that the most effective missionary method lies in reticence, silence, concentrated meditation, so as to give peace to the soul you wish to win; so as not to arouse love precociously; to pray ceaselessly, to be content to scatter a little seed, and allow it to take root and grow in its own time.

A long time passed. One evening the old man asked me: "What do you think of the Bible?"

I answered: "I was left an orphan while I was still a child, and we were very poor. Sometimes I would stand for hours on end in ecstasy outside a baker's shop, gazing with burning desire at the cakes. I would say to myself, 'These are not for me. I shall never be able to eat anything like this.' The Bible brings back these memories. Once again I can see wonderful things, but I know that they are not for me, because I am a Jew. I know that there are Jews who have been converted to Christianity, in order to marry Rumanian girls, or in order to escape anti-Semitic persecution. But I have not yet met a Jew who believes in Jesus."

From that moment Wölfkes became God's instrument to tear the veil from my eyes. He spoke to me in simple words, words that came from the heart, about things that a Jew should have known, but that I did not know: about the fulfilment of the messianic promise in Jesus; of Jesus's tender summons with which he called his people; of the love which God still has for the Jews, for the sake of their forefathers who were bearers of the faith . . .

God opened my heart, so that I was able to believe the gospel.

Wölfkes introduced me to a number of Christian Jews, who were so full of purity—even in their very looks—that I could never till then have believed in the existence of such people.

This humble carpenter provided the first impetus for my conversion. Later, my wife also joined the faith. She brought with her other souls, who in turn brought others, and so on, until a Christian Jewish congregation was formed in Bucharest, which flourished actively for many years.

The existence of this congregation, which was the fruit of his soul's work, was the carpenter's great source of comfort in his last years.

He died during the war. I had to fight on, and later I spent many years in prison. Meanwhile, practically all the Rumanian Christian Jews emigrated, and they have formed congregations in several towns in Israel.

After my release from prison I attended a large meeting of Christians in a village where hundreds of brothers and sisters had come together. I was not strong enough to be able to preach, but I was asked to tell in a few words the story of my conversion. While I was describing it, I noticed that a very old man was weeping. After the meeting was over, I started to talk to him. He told me that his name was Pitter, that he was a wheelwright, and that it was he who had brought Wölfkes to the faith. Up to then he had believed that all he had ever accomplished in life was to convert a carpenter. Now he realised that he had contributed greatly to the struggle of the Christian Jews for Jesus in Israel, and that he was a great-grandfather in the faith to many souls.

Hitler killed the Jews. German Christians worked to save the Jews. Here were two different worlds. When I think of these humble Germans, who gave me spiritual birth, I am reminded of what Martin Luther wrote to a Jew by the name of Jesel:

"Would it not be right for you to believe that because Gentiles and Jews have always been mortal enemies, we should not even bend the knee to the best of your kings? So much the less to such a Jew, crucified and cursed, unless this revealed the power and work of God, He who with His strength implanted them in our proud Gentile hearts? You Jews would never worship as Lord a dead Gentile who had been crucified or suffered some other shameful death. For this reason you must not consider us Christians to be fools or geese, but you must one day realise that God will lead you out of the misery which you have endured for more than fifteen hundred years—but this he will not do unless you, together with us Gentiles, accept the beloved Jesus, the crucified."

It is a miracle, with no logical explanation, that even amid the fierce anti-Semitism of Hitler's oppression, there were Germans who believed with all their hearts in the crucified Jew as their Saviour, some of them suffering profoundly because the Jews remained indifferent to Him who is the glory of His people Israel.

Rabbis help to dispel my doubts

Though the rabbis are the shepherds of the Jewish people, I had reached my twenty-seventh year without experiencing their leadership. They did not lead me into green pastures, nor by still waters. I do not know what other business they had; but they did not come to find the lost sheep. It might have been just my misfortune. There probably are rabbis who fulfil their duty.

Sometimes I would go to the synagogue, but I understood nothing of what was chanted there. Nor did the other Jews. The cantors realised that we could not understand Hebrew, but still they sang for hours on end in that language. It was obvious that they cared little if we knew anything about God. Indeed I wonder whether they themselves were "in God". Reformed Judaism was unknown in Rumania.

But I must not be unfair: Christian priests and pastors made just as little effort to seek me out. Priests and pastors generally have other things to do than to look for lost souls where they are to be found, in pubs, in brothels, in gambling dens and among the atheist organisations. I was found by a carpenter, a man whom priests and pastors of the official denominations would have called a "sectarian".

The rabbis did not begin to take an interest in me until their opportunity was past, and I had been sought and found by Israel's great shepherd, Jesus of Nazareth, of whom the Jewish prophets had prophesied.

I was sitting in the house of a rabbi who was one of the out-standing personalities of Rumanian Judaism. I had come to tell him why I believed in Jesus as the Messiah.

Rabbi H. officiated at my marriage: I was married in the synagogue, for the family's sake. He knew then that I was a militant atheist and an anarchic element. Yet he made not the slightest attempt to tell me anything about God. He carried out the ceremony, and that was all.

Now that I had come to God by way of Jesus, he was displeased. He asked me: "What makes you believe in Christ?"

I told him that the prophecy of Isaiah, about eight hundred years before Jesus, had particularly struck me. Reading this prophecy, in the fifty-third chapter, I had the impression that, centuries before the birth of the Saviour, the prophet had fore-seen His entire life, and had depicted it in outline, so that the Jews should recognise Him when he came.

The rabbi stroked his beard, and said to us (my wife was also present): "You should not have read that. That chapter is forbidden to you."

I have subsequently verified this ban in the calendars issued by the Orthodox Jewish congregations, which give the texts from the prophets to be read at public services in the synagogue (the so-called *Haftorahs*). After the part of the Law of Moses called *Shophtim*, Isaiah Chapters 51 and 52 are to be read. On the next Sabbath there follows Chapter 54. Chapter 53 has been omitted. The prophecy about Jesus contained in this chapter is too revealing.

The rabbi urged us: "My children, leave these things alone!"

I answered: "I should like to do so, but the prophecies will not leave me in peace. What other interpretation of this part of the Bible can you give me?"

The rabbi shook his head sadly, and dismissed us without trying to give an explanation. I don't know why.

Several years passed. In 1940, in the course of a pogrom, the Fascists killed two of his sons before his very eyes. They also fired at him, but failed to hit him.

Rabbi H. personally conducted his sons' burial service. It

greatly moved all those present to see him place his hands on both coffins, and to hear him begin his sermon with the words of the psalmist: "The Lord is righteous in all His ways, and holy in all His works" (Ps. 145. 17).

Thousands of Bucharest Jews were present in the cemetery: I was also there, though I was ostracised because of my Christian faith. I stood by myself at the entrance to the chapel. After the ceremony was over, as the rabbi was leaving, supported by two Jews, he caught sight of me, and called to me from a distance: "Richard!" He embraced me in the sight of all who were present. Among the thousands of Jews he had chosen me to whom to pour out his sorrow.

I have met him several times since then, and he has always listened to me lovingly when I have told him about my faith. I have never tried to force myself upon him. The man who had organised the murder of over a hundred Jews in the Jilava Forest, and hanged about forty others in the municipal slaughterhouse under a sign "Kosher Meat", had been a Greek Orthodox priest. It is difficult to bring a Jew to Christianity.

The other rabbi with whom I spoke about Jesus at the beginning of my belief, while I was still doubting and suffering intellectual scruples, was Rabbi R. from Satu-Mare.

I met him one evening in a synagogue. When I mentioned the Saviour to him, he answered: "If you are prepared to listen quietly to me for half an hour, I will free you from this delusion."

I answered: "I am prepared to listen to you, not for half an hour, but for many days."

He came home with me, and we agreed to read the New Testament together, so that he should have an opportunity of interrupting me from time to time, and of pointing out anything that was incorrect. We read together from eight in the evening until one o'clock next morning. He listened attentively, interrupting me from time to time, always with the same exclamation: "*Oi, vi shein, oi vi shein! Dus hob ich nicht gewist.*" (Ah, how beautiful! How beautiful! I never knew that.) Not once did he contradict. That night he slept at my house. Next day, as we left the house together, he asked me: "Please don't tell anyone in the synagogue what has taken place." I agreed, but added: "I think it should be a point of honour for you to tell the Jews that you consider the New Testament a wonderfully beautiful book."

Rabbi R. did not do that. Later, he moved to Cernauti. A year later I visited him, and found him sitting among his pupils. When I mentioned Jesus to him, he reviled Him with ugly jokes.

During the war he was killed by the Nazis.

When he heard that I was a lost sheep, Rabbi G., who was the successor of a well-known dynasty of miracle-working rabbis, called me to him.

He was an impressive figure, an old man with a white beard and white hair and a lofty forehead. His face shone with goodness. He apologised for having asked me to come to his house; had it not been for his advanced years, he would have come to mine. He asked me what it was that attracted me to Christianity.

I told him briefly the story of my life in sin, and of the peace I had achieved in my conscience through the certainty that my sins are forgiven through Jesus. "Jesus gives me peace in my soul, and joy. I know that He has given peace to millions of people. I know of no evil that He has done. Tell me, Rabbi, why should I abandon Him?"

The rabbi answered: "Jesus did no evil. On the contrary, through Him many people have been saved from the worship of idols and made to know the true God. But you are a Jew. It is your duty to remain in the Jewish religion."

"No," I replied vehemently. "The Jewish religion is false because it is Jewish. Religion must provide men with an exact knowledge of God, and of how man can achieve unity with Him. Just as there can never be a Rumanian theory of physics or a German theory of mathematics, so there can never be a Jewish religion. There is only religion or non-religion. Religion is either true for everyone, or else wrong for everyone.

"In religion we must apply the same principle as in justice. No form of justice to which we give a prefix such as race, caste, class, military, emergency, can be true justice. Justice stands by itself, without any prefix. And for the same reason I accept no prefixes in my belief. I am seeking for contact with God and union with Him. Any religion which has a prefix may prove an obstacle in this search for a union. The Jewish religion binds me to Judaism, the Orthodox and Roman Catholic religions to certain traditions, the Protestant religions to the ideas of their reformers. All these are horizontal unions, not vertical unions with God. It is this vertical union that I seek."

In amazement the rabbi asked me: "I must say with great regret and profound sympathy—not with scorn and malice—that in you I see a person uprooted from his people. Do you not hear within you the voices of your forefathers, calling you back?"

I replied: "Yes, every Jew with sidecurls, the music of a synagogue, the mere sight of the letters in the Hebrew Bible—all these remind me of my forefathers. It is almost like the sight of Abraham with his family, coming to Canaan on his camel. I see before me the scenes from the Bible. I feel myself experiencing the departure of the Jews from Egypt, all their difficulties in the desert, the miraculous event when the Jews received the tablets of the law through Moses. I experience the whole shattering history of my people. But personal biographies and history are one thing, objective truth another.

"The most profound philosophers, politicians and religious thinkers have always offered as objective thinking a system which was nothing but the result of the tragedy of their own personal lives, and they themselves sometimes admit this. Marx wrote in a letter to Engels: 'If Titus had not destroyed my fatherland, I would not have been the enemy of all fatherlands.' One must not allow oneself to be guided by a criterion of this kind in deciding whether to be a patriot or an anti-patriot. And so, even in the religious sphere we must not allow ourselves to be guided by feelings, but we must seek the true religion. That is what I want."

The rabbi shook his head sceptically. "Which *is* the true religion?"

My reply was: "I don't know, yet. But I think I have made a long step towards discovering it, in so far as I have discovered the religion which is certainly incomplete. That is the religion to which I belong by birth. In my opinion it is absurd that religious convictions should depend on the results of a sexual association. A man of the Mosaic faith enters into a union with a woman of the same faith. The child born of this union is regarded as an apostate if he does not believe in Moses. One of his neighbours is a man who is the child of a marriage between a Catholic man and a Catholic woman: he believes that he is compelled to abide by all Catholic dogma. The same applies to a Protestant, or a Mohammedan, or a Buddhist, and the result of this is incomparable confusion. This kind of religion is obviously not the true one, and I do not intend to abide by it."

The rabbi answered: "Jesus did not do what you are doing. He followed in the paths of His forefathers, He kept the sabbath, the laws pertaining to food, and the other laws. He worshipped God in the synagogue. Why do you not do the same?"

I replied: "Jesus was a unique person with a unique vocation. The revelation He made was new; He presented a new and eternally valid truth. In order to win the good will of those who heard Him, He did what every sensible creature does, He clothed His teaching in a form that was acceptable and attractive to His listeners. This is how we can understand His conformism. But through Him the prophecy of Jeremiah, in Chapter 31, is fulfilled: 'Behold, the days come, saith the Lord, that I will make a new covenant with the House of Israel, and with the house of Judah; not according to the covenant that I made with their fathers in the day that I took them by the hand to bring them out of the land of Egypt; which my covenant they brake, although I was an husband unto them, saith the Lord: but this shall be the covenant that I will make with the house of Israel; After those days, saith the Lord, I will put my law in their inward parts, and write it in their hearts; and will be their God, and they shall be my people.'

"We are no longer governed by an old covenant, but by a new revelation, which I can characterise in a few words: freedom in our daily life, and love. One of the renowned Christian teachers, Augustine, declared that the Christian norm in the conduct of his life is: 'Love, and do what you will!' I no longer find Jewish customs imperative or necessary."

To my amazement, the rabbi answered: "I cannot recall such a passage in Jeremiah."

I asked him to take the book from his shelf, and I showed him the reference.

Some rabbis in truth neglect the prophecies because they are continually concerned with the Talmud, the Kabala and numerous commentaries. As a rule, the Books of Moses are the only parts of the Bible they know well.

Among Christian clergy, some of whom have doctors' degrees in theology, it is even worse. I have often come across a profound ignorance of even the simplest Bible texts. If they are Catholics, they are well acquainted with Thomas Aquinas, and if they are Protestants with the works of Barth or Bultmann. They are as a rule ignorant of the theological writings of the great Christian mystics, nor do they know the Holy Scriptures.

The rabbi tried to put an end to our discussion: "I realise that there is no point in arguing. I shall never be able to convince you that you should return to Judaism."

"You do not possess the truth, and therefore you have no confidence either," I replied before I left him. "You have given up all hope of bringing me back to the Mosaic faith, to which I never subscribed. But I shall never give up the hope that one day you will become a disciple of Jesus."

The rabbi shook hands with me hurriedly, and dismissed me.

As a result of what Christians had told me about Jesus, I was still in doubt as to whether He really was the Saviour. The rabbis removed the last shred of doubt on this score, thanks to the complete inability they showed in contradicting the Christian arguments.

The path of belief from reason to the heart

The Jews have an ancient story, so old that Jesus as a boy may have heard it, perhaps from His mother.

One day, a taxidermist caught a beautiful bird, which he intended to kill and stuff. But when he raised his knife to plunge it into its body, a miracle occurred. The bird began to talk to him in human language, saying: "Spare my life, as I have young in my nest. If you will do so, I shall give you three simple pieces of advice, which will prove of great use to you."

The taxidermist thought to himself: "There are many other birds in the woods which I can stuff. But what I am now experiencing is a miracle from God. Who knows what advice I may get?" And so he promised to liberate the bird, if the advice he received was good.

The little bird pronounced three words of wisdom: "If anyone tells you anything absurd, don't believe him, whoever he may be. If you do someone a good turn, you must not regret it afterwards, but rejoice that you have acted benevolently. Do not attempt to reach what is too high for you."

The taxidermist recognised the value of this advice. He had often made the mistake of listening to the counsel of people merely because they were well known. He had often regretted spending money on charity, and he had wasted a great deal of time and energy trying to attain what he could not reach. He released the bird, saying: "Go with God, little bird, because your words were clever."

The bird flew off, to perch on the nearest branch. Then she called out to the man: "Fool! Why did you release me? I have a large diamond in my belly; if you had killed me, you would have found it, and you would have been rich for the rest of your life."

When the taxidermist heard this, he regretted freeing the bird, and began to climb the tree to catch her again. But it is no easy job to catch a bird with bare hands! When he reached the lowest branch, the bird flew off to another. When he reached the second, the bird was yet higher up, and in this way he went on climbing up the tree, until he missed his footing, fell down and broke both his legs.

As he lay groaning at the foot of the tree, the bird hopped down on to the lowest branch and called out to him: "Fool! Did I not give you three good pieces of advice, which you knew in your mind were correct, and admitted with your mouth were good? The first was that you should not believe anything absurd, whoever told you to believe it. How, then, could you be so foolish as to believe that a bird had a diamond in its belly? The second was that you should never regret doing a good turn. You acted charitably by sparing my life. Why did you regret this afterwards? And the third piece of advice was that you should not try to reach something that was too high for you. You know very well that it is impossible to catch a bird with your bare hands. But there is always too great a gap between the human head and the human heart, between the human mouth and the human ear. You saw that my advice was good, but you did not listen to your own words, and you did not believe in the value of your thoughts. A few minutes after approving of my advice, you did the exact opposite of what I had taught you."

Today, we can hear what people are saying and singing on the other side of the world, but our own words are lost, and we live as though we had never pronounced them. Our understanding is one thing, our feelings something quite different. I was to experience the truth contained in this little story.

With my understanding I knew that Jesus is the Saviour; but my life, instead of conforming more and more to His teaching, became, if anything, worse. To my horror, I discovered that I possessed the will to do good, but not the power to carry it out.

"For the good that I would I do not: but the evil which I would not, that I do . . .

"I find then a law, that, when I would do good, evil is present with me . . .

"For I delight in the law of God after the inward man . . . But I see another law in my members, warring against the law of my mind, and bringing me into captivity to the law of sin which is in my members . . ." (Rom. 7.19-23).

There were two aspects to my inner conflict. On the one hand I knew—or rather I felt—instinctively that conversion would mean that I should have to live a life of suffering and conflict. I should have to take my stand against some of my own people, against their customs and ideas which had survived for thousands of years. I knew that—while it was my duty to remain patient and mild—I should have to suffer abuse and condemnation, and yet remain unbowed in every storm.

I should have to be prepared to oppose my people, the people in which I was rooted with all my soul. I heard a voice inside me saying: "Are you, you alone, wiser than all your people? The Jewish nation has fostered so many geniuses, so many mystics, so many men of action, and countless martyrs for the faith of their forefathers! Are all these people wrong, and only you—a small group of Jesus's disciples among the Jewish people—right?" It was not until later that I was compelled to realise that the multitude and the famous men who support a cause are of no argument against God's unequivocal word.

And then, what prospects were in store for me when this conflict had been resolved? Assuming that the Jews were prepared to be converted, where should they go? Later on, I shall relate some of the disappointments I experienced with the various Christian confessions. Very soon I realised that in this world there was no house of the Father to which Israel, the Prodigal Son, could return.

All these thoughts compelled me to compare myself to some Don Quixote going forth to a meaningless battle. The sin in me exploited the difficulties, preventing me from being born anew. "Eat, drink and enjoy yourself, for youth is fleeting," it always whispered.

It was in this period of conflict that I experienced the presence of Jesus for the first time. I cannot say that I saw Him: He had no outward appearance, but He was present. This phenomenon was repeated for several days running. It was at midday; I had cast myself down on a sofa. The tears ran down my cheeks: it was as though I heard a voice calling me—not with words—but if I were to describe what I felt, it would be something like this: "Come! I will give you happiness. All your sins will be forgiven. Unspeakable joys await you." My wife was at my side, saddened by the conflict within me, which she shared with all her heart. But I answered: "No, no, I shall not come. You are calling me to tread a heavy path. Too much renunciation, too many sufferings await me. I do not want them. Depart from me!"

May God forgive me if, without wanting to do so, I appear to blaspheme: I had the impression that Jesus, the Lord of Heaven, was kneeling before me, a sinner, instead of the other way round. And He begged me to turn to God. I felt that my heart would burst with the weight of His sorrow, but I could not. My answer was always "No".

I did not accept, because I was evil. Nevertheless, I believe that some sermons and Christian books on which I fed my soul at that time were in part responsible for the answer I gave. In these sermons and books the picture of Jesus was falsified: He

was shown as a police officer, demanding rigid obedience to
hundreds of laws. These laws started by insisting that one should
renounce smoking and the wearing of jewellery, and ended by
insisting that one should sacrifice one's life for Him. The
emphasis was on all these "don'ts", and on our duty to give to
God, instead of depicting Him as the giver of gifts of immeasure-
able worth—forgiveness of sins, peace of heart, communion with
God, truth, life in the Light, the Spirit which gives power and
holiness, the joy in fighting the good fight—with the angels
fighting on your side—an eternal life of glory, and so much
more—and all these gifts bestowed without any conditions.

In one of the Talmudic writings, we read that any love
which depends on a thing ceases when that thing ceases to
be; but a love which is not dependent on a thing, never ceases.
If the salvation which Jesus gives us depended on a state of soul,
it would not endure because the state of our soul varies. The
salvation bestowed by Jesus is free, unconditional; it does not
depend on what is in us, or on what we do. It springs from His
loving character, and for this reason it is eternal.

Christian preaching is often bound up with "don'ts" and
demands, and this gave me a false idea of Jesus. But what
restrained me, more than anything else, was the fact that I was
in bondage to sin: love of money, love of illicit pleasures, hatred,
evil, dishonesty, and much besides. I continued to commit
grave and gross sins, even after I was intellectually convinced
that Jesus is the Saviour.

But what Luther said happened in my life: "Sins do not
destroy the saints,* but they stifle only those who are without
God." There are two reasons for this. The first is that the saints
believe in Christ, in whom they are completely absorbed, and
through whom they rise again (even though in their ignorance
they do many things for which, without God, they would be
condemned), and in whom they are preserved. They do not fall
into mischief, as Solomon says (Prov. 24.16). For those who have
never experienced it, it is inconceivable how great is the power

---

* The word "saint" is not used here in the sense that the Roman Catholics
use it to describe a person who has been canonised, but is a title which,
according to the New Testament, all believers bear.

that faith will give, especially where sin is concerned. Those who are without God sin, even if they were to do the deeds of all the saints. The other reason is that the saints, through faith, realise that they depend only on God's mercy: yet they recognise in the depths of their hearts that their deeds are sinful and futile. This humility and this testimony prevents them from being destroyed by their sin, ignorance or evil, because God cannot abandon such humble people. The mercy he shows to those who confess their guilt is all the greater. This was true of Bernard of Clairvaux, when he exclaimed in his grief: "I have wasted my time, for I have lived a life which deserves condemnation!" It was true of Augustine when he said: "Woe to the lives of all men, however holy they may be, should they be judged without mercy!"

The seed which God planted in my heart was not corrupted by visible sins. The inner man continued to grow; and the Holy Ghost triumphed by transplanting my belief from my reason to my heart.

Isac Feinstein and my rebirth

The man who was to play a very special role in all this was Isac Feinstein, one of the most glorious triumphs the grace of Jesus has won among the Jewish people.

At the time of his conversion he was a minor business executive. One evening, in a Christian gathering, he heard the message of Jesus. Immediately he believed. When he came home, he ran up to the bedroom of his parents, who had already retired for the night, woke them up and exclaimed: "I have found the Messiah!"

From that evening he never wavered in his faith, although he encountered great resistance from his family.

His father, a pious Jew, tried to persuade him to deny Jesus. When this proved unsuccessful, he arranged for the ceremony to be carried out which is prescribed by rabbis in cases of this kind. He declared that his son was dead, carried out a symbolic burial with a coffin in which the branch of a tree was placed, tore his clothes, and wept for his son together with his family, sitting on the floor for seven whole days.

All this time the "dead man" rejoiced in a life which was richer than ever, and he grew in grace and knowledge of God.

After he had been a Christian for some time, he prepared to work heart and soul to spread the gospel among the Jews of Rumania. He took a missionary training in Poland, and on his return to Rumania he entered the service of the Norwegian Israel Mission in Galatz.

This man had an unlimited capacity for work. He published a periodical for adults and one for children, as well as countless Christian pamphlets. He preached all over the country, and wrote numerous letters. He became an outstanding personality among the disciples of Jesus in Rumania, a pillar of God's temple.

But in order to assess a man's real value, one must consider the conclusion of his career. Napoleon wrote: "Great men are meteors which are extinguished in order to give light to the universe." But Napoleon gave no light to the universe; on the contrary, he caused the world to bleed and weep, by creating a science without which the world would have been a better place—the science of warfare.

Meteors do not bring light to the universe: even the biggest meteor merely leaves behind briefly a transient stream of light which the vast universe does not even notice. The people who are the light of the world are those who add sacrifice to sacrifice—just as islands are formed of coral, one tiny body upon the other. They are the people who are seldom known, who generally remain anonymous, who play a humble role in raising children, running a household, in art, in political, economic and academic life; these are the people who shine with truth, love and faith, shedding a light on those around them. Feinstein was such a burning light.

Feinstein was still a young man when war broke out. He was thirty-seven years old, a pastor in a Jewish-Christian congregation he had formed in Jassy, and from here his benevolent activity spread over the whole country.

The atmosphere in Jassy was infected with anti-Semitism, with the ever-present overhanging threat of a pogrom. Feinstein was on a short visit to Bucharest, staying in my flat. I suggested that he should not return to Jassy, where death lay in wait for him. "We could send a Rumanian brother to bring your wife and your six small children back to Bucharest."

He answered: "The shepherd's duty is to die together with his flock. I know they will kill me, but I cannot abandon my brethren. I am returning to Jassy."

A few days after his return, on June 28th, 1941, the pogrom broke loose. The number of Jews killed was eleven thousand. Rumanians, too, were killed if they looked like Jews. Christian Jews were also killed by the Fascist authorities and by the incensed populace, who maintained that the country was waging a holy crusade.

Feinstein was among those arrested. He was taken at first to the police prison. Criminals who were in prison at that time have recounted since their release that Feinstein told the Jews not to have any illusions. He knew that they would be killed, and he exhorted them to be converted in order that they might prepare to meet their God.

Thousand of Jews were crammed together in sealed cattle-trucks, and sent off beneath the scorching sun, without a drop of water, with the result that most of them were suffocated. Among these was Feinstein. The few survivors were interned in a concentration camp.

Some of these related how, when Feinstein realised that death was at hand, he turned to a rabbi who was standing near him and said: "It is time for us to sing the psalms!"

He died while the rabbi was reciting the psalms aloud, and Feinstein was explaining what they foretold about Jesus. When death came with suffocation, his head was resting on the rabbi's shoulder. The rabbi himself died only a few minutes later—a Mosaic Jew and a Christian Jew were the victims of the same hatred, the hatred which in Rumania was doubly vile because it masqueraded behind the name of "Christian".

Not a single man from the Jewish-Christian congregation in Jassy survived; all were killed in the pogrom. Only a few girls escaped with their lives.

I have described Feinstein's death—a martyr of the Christian faith who was of the Jewish race.

This outstanding man, who had a shepherd's heart such as I have seldom come across since, played an important role in the spiritual crisis through which I passed.

He used to visit our home and I would talk to him about my sin, and how impossible it was for me to rid myself of it. He explained that Jesus's words, "Judge not", referred not only to other people, but also to myself. "In spiritual matters any form of self-diagnosis is wrong. When you raise your right hand in front of a mirror, the mirror will show you that you are raising your left hand, and when you stand in front of a mirror with your face towards the south, it will show you standing with your face towards the north. Your conscience mirrors your spiritual condition, and for that reason your conscience will distort reality unless it is illuminated by the Holy Spirit.

"The Gospels tell us of two men who went up to the temple to pray: one was a Pharisee, the other a publican. The first man diagnosed himself, and was sincere when he came to the conclusion that he was good because he fasted often, and gave generously to the temple. The other man did the same thing, but he discovered that he was sinful because he lived on ill-gotten gains. The self-diagnosis of both men was wrong. God does not take account of what is seen on the surface, but of what is hidden in the hearts of men. In the depths of his heart the first man was a proud person, condemning others, while the publican was humble, and confessed his sin."

"Don't judge yourself," was the advice Feinstein always gave me. "Don't distress yourself, don't worry yourself about your sin. It is written, 'Take no thought for your soul' [Matt. 6.25, in the original Greek version]. The care of the soul is Jesus's concern. Just tell Him quite simply about your sin, and from that moment it will be His concern to deal with it.

"Our own understanding is the hypocrite whom Jesus reproaches for observing the mote in his brother's eye, which is the sin of brother flesh, a result of our heredity, a faulty upbringing, the pressure of social circumstances, the influence of the devil, and a large number of imponderable factors. But the hypocrisy of the understanding lies in the fact that it does not come down from the lofty pinnacle from which it judges all things and all men, in order to observe the beam in its own eye—its false criteria of truth, its selfishness, its passion, its ignorance of condemning oneself, the fact that it is not to be trusted. The proof that the beam is in the eye of reason, is that reason cannot remove the mote from its brother's eye, but is merely content to reproach him for it, and make life intolerable for him.

"Try to conquer sin by making an indirect attack on it. In the heart, Satan is strong, because he provides the heart with pleasures. Here it is difficult to overcome him. In the reason he is weak, because here he creates only difficulties. 'Be ye transformed by the renewing of your *mind*,' says Paul (Rom. 12.2). Jesus fought His battle at Golgotha, which in Aramaic means 'The Place of the Skull'. This is where you, too, must fight your battle. Make every thought a captive, in obedience to Christ. Accept Him as the criterion of truth. Superficial truth, which is easily grasped, will not change men's hearts. The daily truth which you ponder deeply, which you contantly chew over until it is transformed within you, will undoubtedly change your life.

"The Talmud tells the story of the rabbi Akiba, who as a young man was both ignorant and profane, and whose intelligence was not fully developed. But he had a wife who had great faith in God, and who asked her husband to sanctify himself and become a teacher of the law. Akiba used to object: 'But I have no talent for this.' She took him to a well, on the parapet of which the rope had worn away the stonework, so that there was a small depression. 'Can you see this groove in the stone?' she said to him. 'The rope is much softer than the stone, yet for many years it has worn away at the hard stone, and formed a depression. Be like the rope—up and down, up and down, always the same motion: the Scriptures and prayer, the Scriptures and prayer. Even if the heart and mind are as hard as stone, they will eventually be penetrated by the Word of God.'

"Akiba listened to the words of his wife, and became one of the great lights of Judaism; he was finally crowned with a martyr's death. Do as he did! Be zealous in thinking what is right and Christian, and you will not need to run away from sin, for sin will run away from you."

It was thanks to Feinstein, who had a beautiful singing voice, that I was for the first time in my life introduced to Bach's hymn "O sacred Head". The song went straight to my heart.

One afternoon in 1937, the day before Yom-Kippur, the great

Jewish day of repentance and fasting, I was in Feinstein's office. My soul was greatly troubled, as indeed it had been from my earliest childhood years. I said to Feinstein: "The demands of Christianity are too extreme, they are impossible to fulfil. It is written in the Bible that he who says that he is Christ's must also live as Jesus lived. But is that possible? It's like asking a wolf to live like a lamb, and then condemning it for not succeeding. Since I have not been Christ through all eternity, since I was not born of a virgin, since I have not had Jesus's especially chosen and holy upbringing, since I have no clear perception of spiritual realities, nor do I have His mind, since God's angels are not continually ascending and descending upon me, since I do not live in celibacy, nor am I a carpenter—how, then, should I be able to live as He did? Must the snail run like the hare? From the little I have seen of Christians so far, conversion for some means merely making Jesus an interesting subject of conversion; it does not mean that they are converted to be a Jesus in miniature. At any rate I have not seen people of Jesus's type."

Feinstein answered with his inimitable smile: "Don't allow yourself to be guided by what you see, because it is possible that you do not see very well. The Jews who lived two thousand years ago didn't see in Jesus anything that made Him worthy of honour, despite the fact that He was the incarnation of God. Unless a man is born anew he cannot see God's kingdom, even though it is perfectly incarnate in the man who is standing face to face with him.

"But is it not expected of us that we should be like Jesus, that we should live like Him? The verse in St. John's Epistle to which you referred—'He that saith he abideth in Him ought himself also to walk' (1 John 2.6)—does not make our belief absurd, it is merely a warning to those who go round proudly declaring: 'I am in Christ.'

"There was once a country in which there were two great painters. The country was divided into two: one half of the population preferred one painter, the other part preferred the other. The king of that country was asked to pronounce his verdict. He had the marble hall in his palace divided into two by a curtain; then he summoned the first painter, and ordered him to paint anything he liked on one wall of the hall. He summoned the other painter and ordered him to paint on the opposite wall. The first painter, who was just as talented as he was conceited, immediately set to work and painted a great many beautiful things, assisted by his pupils. The painter on the other side was a humble man. He said to his pupils: 'It is foolish for me to try to compete with my excellent rival. I cannot paint as he can. But I shall ask you to do something else. Stay here from morning to evening, and polish the marble until it shines.' And so it was done. On one side of the curtain they painted, and on the other side they polished the wall. On the appointed day, the king came to see the work of the two painters. He admired the work of the first, and declared that he had never seen more beautiful pictures. Then he ordered the curtain to be pulled to one side, so that he might see what the other painter had done. He stepped back in amazement. The pictures painted by the first artist were reflected in the marble which had been polished by the other, and their beauty was dazzling. The second painter received the prize.

"The moral of this story is very simple. Only a very proud person could imagine himself capable of living like Jesus. The commandment to live like Jesus did, like all the other commandments in the Bible, was not given to us so that we should fulfil it, but merely so that we should understand—as a result of our constantly unsuccessful attempts—that it is impossible for us to accomplish it, and so that it should reveal to us the depth of our sinfulness. We should not attempt to live like Jesus, but we should daily 'polish' our hearts by concentrated meditation and by faith, and then the beauty of Jesus will be reflected in us—it will give a still more beautiful picture than the picture of His own life, because the living Christ, incarnate in a human being who had been broken and had gone astray, is more beautiful than the Christ incarnate born of a virgin."

"No, no!" I cried, with tears in my eyes. "I do not want a Jesus who has been calculated, explained, and believed in, but a real Jesus. And the hope of ever having this Jesus seems to me to be an impossible ideal." So saying, I ran out of Feinstein's office, without taking leave of him.

He ran after me; I could not escape from him. I went into a shop—he followed me inside. He was so insistent that he per-

suaded me to accompany him that very evening to a prayer
meeting which was being held by a small group of Christians in
Bucharest, in the hall of the Anglican Mission to the Jews.

There, after most of the congregation had offered up prayers,
I was involuntarily lifted up by the Spirit. I was astonished to
hear myself for the first time praying aloud in a public gathering.
I heard my own words, but they did not seem to be words that
I had formulated. They sprang from the depths of my soul, to
which as a rule my ego cannot gain access. Proof that the depths
had been stirred was the fact that I prayed in Yiddish—the
centuries-old language of my people in their suffering, a
language which in other circumstances I never spoke.

I consider the eve of Yom-Kippur 1937 as the day of my
rebirth, because—this is obvious—the teaching of Jesus cannot
be written clearly on a page which already bears some other
writing. What is required is a complete break with the past, and
a completely new beginning, the starting point of which is a
constant and uncompromising siege of one's thinking.

The person who was most astonished at this change, a man
who had once been a militant atheist and an active participant in
the worst anarchic disturbances, was myself. My will was not
free when this change occurred. My hand was forced. Everything
is of the grace of God.

I believe that just as there is in nature a biological timetable
which governs the time when a young bird has to emerge from
its egg and when it has to migrate to another country, and to
return at a definite date, and just as there is a biological timetable
in man's physical life, so there is a spiritual timetable which is
also determined in the same way. For every person who is chosen
by God, there is a particular foreordained hour when he discovers the Son of God, who has always been in him but who
has waited patiently for the moment when He is to reveal
Himself. In that particular hour, internal and external factors,
which have been prepared a long time ago, come together in
order to produce this rebirth.

Difficulties with some Christian traditions

I had determined to be faithful to Jesus. But the man who has made this decision must discover the true face of Jesus among the countless forgeries that have accumulated in the course of time; he must decide for himself on one version of this face, in order to be able to serve Him wholly and entirely, and without doubting that he has chosen the right confession. I was very interested in the difference between the confessions: I was anxious to be well-informed before I commenced my life as a Christian.

But it was not easy to make a choice.

Throughout Church history there has been much vexation of spirit, and striving for riches. In Jassy there is a Greek Orthodox church which is so crammed with golden ikons, candlesticks, and vessels that the only way they have discovered of guarding all this wealth has been not to open the church for services. In this way the words of St. Augustine have been fulfilled when he says that religion has produced riches and fortunes, but the daughters have consumed their mother.

There was striving for fame; there was the blind rage felt by a theologian when he was contradicted or eclipsed by one who was more attractive than himself; there was a storing up of feuds and hatreds which lasted a whole lifetime—even several centuries—without any respect for the beautiful proverb from the Babylonian Talmud: "The sun has set and the day is clear." The teaching of God has been made into a "crown to glorify oneself with, and a spade to dig with," as the Talmud says. The word of God has been used to promote transient political interests, and to stifle the truth with misdeeds.

The different ways of thinking, which could have led to a very fruitful competition in the study of the word of God if only the royal law, the law of love, had been kept, combined with repulsive sins to replace the Church, the one Church, with many confessions, some of which allow themselves to be guided by the arrogant slogan formulated by Hitler: "Where we are, there is no room for others."

Between the various confessions flow the rivers of blood shed during religious persecutions, not only in the past but also in our own generation. During the last war the Rumanian Orthodox Church violently persecuted not only Jews, at the killing of whom priests assisted, but also what they call "sectarians", that is to say, Baptists, Brethren, Adventists and the like, thousands of whom were imprisoned.

The convert seeks in vain for "the House of the Father", the Church that was founded by Jesus. In its place he finds many other churches with barbarian names, which the one-time carpenter, Jesus, would not even have understood: Catholic, Orthodox, Lutheran, Baptist, and many others.

As far back as the fourth century St. Epiphanius, when he spoke about the Audians—members of a sect, founded by a certain Audius, who insisted that God has a body like that of a man—declared: "It is a terrible thing that a member of the Church should change the name of the Christians while the Church only rejoices when Christians bear the name of Christ and reject all other designations. But instead of bearing the name of Christ, they bear the name of the founder of their sect, and as a sign they have the name of a human being. This is inadmissible."

This warning went unheeded: we still have confessions that bear strange names, and the soul of the bride wanders around like one who has lost her way, while she seeks her bridegroom.

One wonders whether the astronauts would have ventured into space if twenty scientists had submitted their calculations, all with divergent results, and had told them contradictory things from the world of physics. They were launched into space, relying on the accurate data of science and mathematics. But how should we fly to the Throne of God, when the trumpets of the different confessions produce such discordant noises, and each one destroys confidence in everything that the others have said?

It was in this labyrinth that I had to find my way.

Let me describe a few episodes. I trust that the reader will forgive me if, in doing so, I cite some examples of human frailty. One of Melanchthon's biographers wrote: "Anyone who considers it shameful to discover anything worth criticising in great and famous men, entertains too high an opinion of human beings, since God alone is privileged to be faultless. Human nature is incapable of this." As the reader will soon discover, I find a great deal of good, too, in the various confessions and their leaders, just as my experience with rabbis was not always unfavourable.

I was once in Sinaia, with one of my brothers-in-law, who was later converted. We were visiting the Orthodox monasteries in the town. It was the day after Easter Monday. We knocked at one of the gates, and an old monk admitted us.

"What do you want?" he asked.

"Father, we have come to ask what we must do to be saved."

"You are unlucky, because today of all days I have drunk too much."

"It is Easter, Father. Have you not found a worthier way of celebrating Easter than by getting drunk?" I asked, no longer concerned with my original errand, which was to seek enlightenment from him.

"Young man," the monk answered, with a merry laugh, "I have drunk according to the commandment of the Scriptures, since I have not drunk alone but in company with two or three other brethren. For it is written that 'where two or three are gathered together in my name, there am I in the midst of them,' as the Saviour said."

I had come to learn, but I was now compelled to assume the role of teacher, and to teach him the most elementary things.

"Father, I believe that when Jesus said that He would be together with His people, where two or three were gathered, he was referring to a gathering of people who had come to do good deeds or to pray, not to get drunk."

With a humility which impressed me, he answered: "Do you know, young man, you are right?" and he invited us into his cell, as we had been standing talking on the threshold.

This monk was a man accustomed to drinking. The wine had not gone to his head, and it was possible to talk to him.

I repeated my question: "What should I do to be saved?"

"Are you rich?"

"I am neither rich nor poor. I have what I need. But why do you ask?"

"The rich man is easily saved. He gives money to the Church and to the needy, and he goes to Heaven. But it is difficult for a poor man to be saved, since he has nothing to give."

The man to whom I had gone in order to learn the way of Jesus was saying the very opposite of what Jesus had taught.

I asked him: "But what role does Jesus play in our salvation?"
He answered: "I know nothing about that."

Once again I asked: "But Father, do you not say in the liturgy: 'This is my blood, the blood of the new covenant, which is shed for many for the forgiveness of sins'? Is it not true that the blood the Saviour shed on the Cross cleanses us of our sins?"

The old monk started up and exclaimed: "Do you know, young man, you are very enlightened?"

There was obviously no point in asking him to guide me. A Christian Jew, who was still trying to find the way, had helped the old monk to take the first steps along this very road.

I was in the office of Bishop X. At his side were two of his advisers, priests. I told him who I was, and of my wish to be guided in the labyrinth of the many different confessions.

When he heard that I was a Jew, the bishop burst out laughing: "Ha, ha, ha. Dumb Jew! Have you ever heard a more presumptuous dirty Jew, wanting to be a Christian?" The two priests at his side joined deferentially in his laughter.

I was prepared for a reception of this kind. Feinstein had told me of another bishop who raised his crozier to strike him when he heard that he was a Christian Jew.

This was not surprising. Bishops and priests had been nourished on the so-called holy tradition, on the writings of the Church fathers; that is, if they had ever read them. But many of the "holy Church fathers", often so-called quite fraudulently, were rabid anti-Semites.

St. Cyril personally conducted a pogrom against the Jews. The houses of Jews were destroyed, and their inhabitants driven out of Alexandria. As an excuse for this "holy" bishop, it may be mentioned that he did not persecute only Jews: he behaved just as outrageously against his own colleagues in his see. He was also involved in the murder of the philosopher Hypatia in a church.

St. John Chrysostom declared: "I know that a great many Christians have a certain reverence for the Jews and their ceremonies. For this reason I consider it my duty to root out opinions of this kind, which are fraught with danger. I have previously declared that the synagogue is worth no more than a theatre." He then proceeds to call the synagogue "a whore-house", "a den of thieves", and so on, and concludes: "In their shamelessness and greed the Jews exceed even the pigs and the goats . . . The Jews are possessed of demons and delivered into the hands of unclean spirits. Instead of greeting them and doing them the honour of addressing a few words to them, you must turn your backs on them, and avoid them like the pestilence and a plague to humanity."

St. Ambrose insisted that the Jews, as the enemies of Christ, cannot claim just treatment—they are not under the protection of the law. Ambrose threatened to excommunicate the Emperor if he sided with some Jews who had been unjustly treated. The mild Bernard of Clairvaux was furious, and lodged an official protest, when Anacletus II was elected Pope, because one of his grandparents had been a Jew. The doctrine held by another Church father is briefly set out in the Abbé Gayragand's book on *The Antisemitism of St. Thomas Aquinas:* "The Jew is the enemy of Jesus. In a Christian country Jews must be treated as a foreign and hostile race, and must be deprived of every political right accorded to the citizens. They must, however, be allowed to practise their religion without being punished for it, since they are living testimonies to our Lord's suffering. For this reason they are scattered about in all the countries of the world, suffering just punishment for their terrible crime, so that they can witness to our redemption." Until recently, every Good Friday, worshippers in the Catholic Church prayed for the "perfidious Jews". This formula has now been omitted from Roman Catholic services, but in the anti-Semitic writings of their Church fathers future priests continue to imbibe this doctrine.

It was normal for the disciples of the "holy" fathers to laugh at me. In so doing they were following in the footsteps of their teachers.

I rose from the chair in which I was sitting, strode over to the bishop's desk, and struck it with my clenched fist. "Aren't you ashamed of yourself? You are a Christian bishop, and yet you laugh at a Jew because he believes in Jesus. What nationality was Jesus? And His Mother? And the Apostles? You fill your churches with pictures of 'dirty' Jews, yet you laugh at Jews. Do you not fear God?"

The bishop was a little man, and I am very tall. When his advisers saw me gesticulating violently, they were afraid that I might strike him, and they got ready to restrain me. But the bishop waved them aside, and called out: "Stop! Let him be! There is good in this young man. I wish to speak with him."

The conversation which then ensued was calm. He congratulated me on the new path on which I had set my feet. He was also anxious that I should win over other Jews to Christ. But there would have been no point in asking him in any detail about this path.

The Orthodox priest in the parish to which I belonged was sitting in the yard in front of his house. When I told him I was a Jew who believed in Jesus, he set his dogs on me.

I could describe numerous encounters of this kind with Orthodox priests, but it would be pointless. Such men have no right to the title of shepherd, instituted by Jesus to lead the Church of Christ. Anyway, I am convinced that Jesus never instituted a separate clergy. All disciples of Jesus are priests.

I have studied the dogma taught by the Greek Orthodox Church, and have found that it contains a great many falsehoods. Personally, it would never have occurred to me to join this Church. Its ritual used at the baptism of a Jew compels the convert to spit three times and declare: "I deny, curse and spit on Jews," in other words on his own parents, brothers and sisters and all his family. I know of cases where the person who was being baptised fainted during the ceremony when compelled to pronounce this curse. One Jewish man was quite incapable of uttering a word.

Furthermore, as soon as the Fascist regime had been established in Rumania, the Holy Synod of the Greek Orthodox Church declared that no Jew should be received into the Church. What wretched person can have placed this barrier in the way of the Jews, to prevent them entering the Church of Jesus? He, after all, once said: "I am not sent but to the lost sheep of the house of Israel" (Matt. 15.24). In fairness, I must say that I have since met Orthodox priests who were saints, but my early experiences were bad.

In my search for the right Church the facts which proved to my satisfaction which was not the true Church proved an important step in the right direction.

People call me a Lutheran. The Lutheran Church is a remarkable one, a Church which exists against the wishes of the man who founded it.

This is what Luther wrote: "To establish and to follow many sects and multitudes in the faith is tantamount to dividing God into many gods, and to giving Him many names. A sect is nothing but a schism, which is forbidden by God, from the true, universal, invisible Church, an act committed by an earthly being. I do not approve of the doctrine and the people that are called Lutheran, and yet I must suffer that God's word should be mocked in this way by my name. I pray that my name may not be mentioned, and that men should call themselves not Lutherans but Christians. Why should I, a putrid bag filled with maggots, deserve that the Children of Christ should bear my wretched name? No one must say: 'I am a Lutheran' or 'I am a Papist', for neither Luther nor the Pope died for us, and neither of them was our teacher, but Christ alone was our teacher. For this reason we should call ourselves Christians."

In his table talks he said: "Let the Devil take Luther, if he can. Christ shall live."

Nevertheless, the Lutheran Church exists, and from Luther it has inherited anti-Semitic doctrines which come to light as soon as appropriate conditions exist.

You cannot ask a Jew to be pro-Hitler. How can you expect him to be a Lutheran, when Luther wrote in a letter to his wife, who also despised the Jews profoundly: "I must now deal with the expulsion of the Jews. Count Albrecht is their enemy, and he has also opposed them, but as yet no one is dealing with them. If it is God's will, I shall assist Count Albrecht from the pulpit, and I too shall oppose them. I am drinking Naumburger beer . . . and I like it very much."

I have selected a mild passage; there are others in which he openly incites his readers to kill Jews—just as he had incited them to kill Catholics, peasants and Anabaptists. He criticised the Inquisition because it had not subjected his former friend, Thomas Münzer, to sufficient torture.

When I was converted, the bishop of the Lutheran Church in Rumania was a pro-Hitler man by the name of Städel, who preached a combination of Christianity, racialism and National Socialism. Anyone who entered the vestry of a Lutheran church was greeted with a "Heil Hitler"—"Heil to the murderer of millions of Jews".

In truth, this Church did not represent Christ either.

The Lutheran churches in Scandinavia and Holland rose gallantly to the occasion during the difficult years experienced by the Jews, and this is to their credit. But in doing so they were obeying another Luther.

Luther was something of a split personality. He also wrote some very beautiful things about the Jews: "We should not treat the Jews so badly, because among them are future Christians. If we were to live in a Christian manner and bring them to Christ with goodness, this would be the right thing to do. Who will become a Christian when he sees Christians acting in such an unchristian manner towards men? Not so, dear Christians. Let us tell them the truth with goodness. If they do not want it, give them peace. We give peace to so many Christians who do not care about Christ and do not listen to His words ... If I had been a Jew and had seen such fools and idiots leading and teaching the Christian faith, I would rather have become a pig than a Christian. If the apostles, who also were Jews, had treated us, the Gentiles, as we treat the Jews, no Gentile would ever have become a Christian."

I will not tell of my experiences with Catholicism, which is changing so much just now, even beyond what Luther would have hoped. The Second Vatican Council has absolved the Jews of the guilt of killing Jesus. The Crucified had absolved them long before with the words, "No man taketh [my life] from me, but I lay it down of myself" (John 10.18). The fathers of the Vatican

Council would have done better to have apologised for killing the Jews over the centuries. To be fair, I should add that it is not only Christians who have hated and killed Jews. It has also sometimes been the other way round. Jews such as Trotsky in Russia, Rakosi in Hungary and Anna Pauker in Rumania killed many Christians, though not from religious motives. And in any case, hatred on one side is no excuse for hatred on the other.

As time went on, all the great Christian confessions seemed to me to be a Babel. They bore no resemblance to the Church that Jesus left behind, as described in the Acts of the Apostles: "And the multitude of them that believed were of one heart and of one soul: neither said any of them that ought of the things which he possessed was his own; but they had all things common. And with great power gave the apostles witness of the resurrection of the Lord Jesus, and great grace was upon them all. Neither was there any among them that lacked: for as many as were possessors of lands or houses sold them, and brought the prices of the things that were sold, and laid them down at the apostles' feet: and distribution was made unto every man according as he had need" (Acts 4.32–35).

"And they continued steadfastly in the apostles' doctrine and fellowship, and in breaking of bread, and in prayers. And fear came upon every soul: and many wonders and signs were done by the apostles . . . And they, continuing daily with one accord in the temple, and breaking bread from house to house, did eat their meat with gladness and singleness of heart, praising God, and having favour with all the people. And the Lord added to the church daily such as should be saved" (Acts 2.42–43, 46–47).

The great confessions are not the historical successors of the first Church. But the glorious beams from the light of Jesus penetrate even the densest cloud. The gospel breaks through the obstacles which these confessions have set up, and brings salvation to men and women, even to those who follow an erroneous religious system. But the great Church congregations cannot prove effective instruments for the salvation of Israel. Israel will never come to Christ through them.

I felt, and still feel, at home in pietistic circles. Even before I was familiar with the Protestant doctrine of the invisible Church,

I felt a sense of brotherhood with every child of God who had been born anew.

I found brothers and sisters of this kind in "The Army of the Lord", a religious movement within the Orthodox Church. I have met brethren in the faith among Roman Catholic priests and laymen who loved Christ with all their heart, and who did things which I considered wrong, merely because they thought Jesus had prescribed them. In the same way I have met many brethren in the Lutheran Church, and in other Protestant denominations.

Could I ever forget the Greek Orthodox Archimandrite Scriban, who throughout the most violent anti-Semitic persecutions was ready day and night to help us, intervening on our behalf on countless occasions? This man, who had been head of the theological seminary, and most of whose former students were now priests in Bucharest, rebuked those at the head of the Ministry of Culture whenever they made life difficult for us, dismissing us as "dirty Jews". "Is this what I taught you?" he would ask. "Was not Jesus, too, a 'dirty Jew'? And was not the Mother of our Lord a 'dirty Jewess'?"

Among the Lutherans, could I ever forget Bishop Friedrich Müller, the staunch friend of Christian Jews? Or the Norwegian Lutheran clergyman Magne Solheim, head of the Norwegian Israel Mission in Rumania, whose life consisted of nothing but preaching the Word of Christ to the Jews from morning till night, and exerting every effort to help them in their hour of misery?

I have no space to mention the many who acted as these did.

God's children, no matter to what denomination they belonged, were close to me. But I have felt most at my ease among those who have left the great denominations. The hard facts I discovered in the big denominations destroyed the picture of Christ which I had in my heart: I rediscovered this picture in the small Christian groups.

That they were not numerous was no disadvantage as far as I was concerned. I knew that God looks at the heart of man, and not at the number of men. Gregory of Nazianzus declared: "God hath no delight in the majority. Men may be counted by their thousands, but God counts those who accept salvation. Men count insignificant dust, He the instruments of grace."

The pietistic circles which exist within the large denominations and in the sects are the only Christian groups in Rumania whose hands are not soiled with Jewish blood. During the persecutions they assisted, sheltered and rescued Jews. With them it is easiest and best to preach the gospel of Christ to the Jews.

But even among them there were disputes. People of profound faith disagreed among themselves on trivial interpretations of Bible texts.

Believers quarrel over things about which they really know nothing. I have heard that in the Middle Ages there were two believers who were condemned by the Inquisition to be burnt at the stake. They asked to be bound back to back, so that they should not look one another in the eye, as each of them regarded the other as a heretic.

When I heard this story, I thought it was an exaggerated legend. Later on, in prison, I saw people who gave their lives for the same gentle Jesus, but who would not even say "Good morning" to one another, because they belonged to different confessions, or to two different groups within the same confession. We all allow such things to be done, without realising how difficult it will be for us to give an account of the sin we have committed, the sin of making it difficult for those who seek the truth to find it.

I, and other Jews with me, were almost in despair when we tried to find our way through the chaos of religious differences. So far I have not discovered a single Christian organisation which is qualified to tackle the task of preparing the world for the Kingdom of God, and making disciples of all nations. Not a single one of them takes this task seriously, striving towards it according to a definite strategic plan. Many of their efforts are wasted in trivial everyday affairs.

The grace of God helped us to overcome these difficulties, prevented us from losing our way in petty things, and helped us to understand the most important passages in the New Testament, which are so clear, and which alone by their teaching and the practice of this teaching, can bring the Jews to Christ:

"Love is the fulfilling of the law" (Rom. 13.10).

"For all the law is fulfilled in one word, even in this: Thou shalt love thy neighbour as thyself" (Gal. 5.14).

"Therefore all things whatsoever ye would that men should do to you, do ye even so to them: for this is the law and the prophets" (Matt. 7.12).

"Thou shalt love the Lord thy God with all thy heart, and with all thy soul, and with all thy mind. This is the first and great commandment. And the second is like unto it, Thou shalt love thy neighbour as thyself. On these two commandments hang all the law and the prophets" (Matt. 22.37–40).

Despite the fact that the Bible contains numerous passages which state that God commanded circumcision, we know that Paul rejected these holy words, declared the commandment null and void, and wrote: "For in Christ Jesus neither circumcision availeth any thing, nor uncircumcision, but a new creature" (Gal. 6.15).

Should not we, too, be in a position to maintain that the various doctrines which separate us, although they are based on important passages in the Bible, really mean nothing? Instead, we must become "new creatures", people who rebuild their lives on the principle of love, the principle which Jesus gave us an example to follow. If Luther was able to write as much as four centuries ago: "Jesus did not command us to confess, but gave us all liberty, so that he who so desired could avail himself of confession . . . You will not be condemned by God if you do not confess . . . All sacraments must be free; he who does not desire to take the Holy Communion, is entitled by God not to do so," how much more should we in the twentieth century be able to distinguish what is most important in the doctrine of the Bible—love—from what is less important!

The spiritual condition of most Jews, especially young people, may be described as religious indifference. Our theological discussions will surely not help to stir up enthusiasm in them. Our sermons leave them indifferent. Dogmas do not move their hearts.

But it is not in these dogmas that Christianity is to be found. The divine teacher declared that love was the sign by which

His disciples should be recognised. Love leaves no normal person indifferent. The Jews, more than any other people, are thirsting for love. If love were our religion, then their indifference would melt away.

For my own part, after seeking long, to right and left, I have found what I am seeking: my confession is love. My brothers and sisters are all those who love one another, no matter to what denomination they belong. My Lord is Jesus, because He is the incarnation of love. "God is love" and "every one that loveth is born of God" (1 John 4.8, 7).

The Cross of Christ demonstrates the catastrophic results of violating the law of love. Hate crucified truth and the Deity. But at the same time the Cross of Christ is an expression of God's love. Because He loves, Christ takes upon Himself the sins of His murderers, and gives them an opportunity of starting life afresh. This truth, of which I have been allowed to partake, has given me freedom with regard to Christian confessions. I can decide as I like whether I wish or do not wish to join any one of them. They provide the background against which I can exercise the religion of Christ, the religion of love. I am now in a position to worship in churches and assemblies belonging to all confessions. On one and the same day I have preached to Orthodox, Catholics, Lutherans and Pentecostalists.

If you want the truth, you must renounce attitudes and opinions, for every attitude and opinion is also a blind spot which makes you quite incapable of understanding other views and opinions apart from your own. Reality knows itself, because there is spirit in it. Christ is the truth, He is the reality, as it knows itself, without being distorted by being looked at through prisms or from different angles.

Most of the Christian Jews who have subsequently comprised our congregation, have adopted the same interdenominational attitude, despite the fact that our church was formally Lutheran. It was known as "The Church of Love". Pastor Solheim's greeting was "Love". We were the only church in Rumania which—long before the modern ecumenical trend—had men of all denominations kneeling together at the Communion rail.

I am baptised and my wife is won for the Lord

In my wife I have truly found what the Bible describes as "a helper who is his like". There is a certain value in celibacy, but I have also noticed that the competence of many labourers in God's vineyard has been to a large extent due to the fact that they had found an excellent helpmeet in their wives. St. John Chrysostom cannot have known our wives, otherwise this holy father could never have recorded the monstrous statement that "woman is a necessary evil and a deadly fascination".

It is obvious that a woman is a worthy helpmeet if her husband does not browbeat her. We could all take Adam as an example of a good husband. Because of Eve, he lost a paradise, but he did not say a word of reproach to her—whereas we abuse our wives for the merest trifle.

At first, I had difficulties with my wife. When I left home to be baptised, she wanted to commit suicide. My mother fainted when she heard of my decision. Thus I grievously offended two beloved persons when I went to receive my baptism.

At that time I thought it right; I should not advise anyone now to behave in the same way. If one is to witness and to suffer for Christ, it is not right to renounce this for the sake of another person. But some Jews are not so prejudiced against Jesus as they are against baptism. They have too many painful memories of the time when the Inquisitors dragged the Jews by their beards to baptism, under the threat of death. They remember so often that their forefathers cut the throats of their own children, after pronouncing a blessing, in order to save them in this way from forced baptism. All too many Jews allowed themselves to be baptised in order to deny their people. This resulted in an emotional antipathy which can be easily understood. I once knew an old Jewess, who was a faithful follower of Jesus, but who had a strong antipathy against pronouncing the word "baptism". She used to say: "I still have to fulfil this matter."

Complexes of this kind must be carefully dealt with. The duty to love is greater than the duty to be baptised. A person should never be in a hurry to be baptised, before his family is familiar with the idea, and realises what it involves and means. The baptism should not be given unnecessary publicity. We should

witness not for the sign of baptism, but for Him who gave it to
us. It is wrong for a missionary to make it a point of honour to
baptise as many Jews as possible.

But at that time I was of a different mind. I went to my
baptism, leaving behind a weeping wife and a sorrowing mother.

I cannot say into what confession I was baptised. My
baptism took place in the chapel of the Lutheran Norwegian
Israel Mission, the head of which was a Free Church Christian,
Feinstein. The act of baptism was carried out by Brother Ellison,
who had been an Anglican priest, but had left that Church after
being baptised a second time as an adult. He continued nevertheless to conduct services in the Anglican mission. Chaos has
become a commonplace in Christianity, as Jesus's last plea is
ignored: "I pray . . . that they all may be one" (John1 7.21).

It was sufficient for me to know that Ellison was a true-hearted
disciple of Jesus, as were the others who assisted at my baptism.

Two other Jews were baptised with me. One of them,
Blitzstein, was a former Communist. The other was a much
abused man. He was small of stature, and was married to a wife
twice his size, who would assault him every Sunday on his
return from the service. The wretched man continued to attend
our meetings, and was regularly beaten up. After his baptism I
saw to it that his hair was thoroughly dried in front of the stove,
so that she should not realise that he had been baptised. Had
she guessed, she would almost certainly have killed him.

One Sunday, late at night after he had gone to bed, Feinstein
heard a knock at his door, and when he opened it he saw this
brother standing there, as pale as a ghost. He asked what had
happened. The man answered, completely heartbroken: "I have
forfeited my salvation. Today my wife beat me more than ever
before. I could stand it no longer, and I slapped her face." With
a twinkle in his eye, Feinstein replied: "Well, seeing you have
forfeited your salvation, why didn't you at least give her a proper
beating, so that she would have something to remember you by?"
Later on, this Xantippe was also baptised, but she did not remain
steadfast in the faith.

Our baptism took place in a very cordial atmosphere. Ellison,
who was of a high spirituality, warned us: "You have now

received robes of white, and it is your duty to keep them pure." Feinstein, who was more down-to-earth in his approach, also preached: "You are human beings, and you will still sin like all human beings. You will not keep your robes white, but when you do sin, go immediately to Jesus so that He can cleanse you of your stains."

After the ceremony was over, late that evening when everyone had gone to bed, I was unable to sleep. That night I read *The Mysteries of the Cross* by Tohoyiko Kagawa, a Japanese Christian who had devoted not only his entire fortune, but his life and all his knowledge, to help the poor of Japan.

The house where my baptism took place is no longer a chapel. The Communist State now uses it for an entirely different purpose. I am sad to think that I have not been able to see it for many years. Saint Louis, King of France, used to make an annual pilgrimage to the village church at Poissy, where he had been baptised. He used to say: "In this place I received the Crown of Life, while in Rheims I received the royal crown—which has only occasioned me much labour and many cares."

When I returned home after my baptism, I found that my wife had altered. During my absence she had carefully examined her life, and had now taken a big step forward. I still took her with me to secular gatherings, whenever she wanted to go, but she felt more and more out of place there. Late one evening, on our return from a party of this kind, she said to me: "I should like to wake the pastor, so that he can baptise me, and cleanse me of all my impurity."

Not long after this, Ellison baptised her, too. She has been compelled to suffer a great deal since that time. She spent some years in prison; she was separated from her husband for as many years as Jacob served for Rachel. All the sufferings and sorrows of the Christians were hers, too, but she considered that all her worries had been of a few days' duration, because she loved.

JEWS WHO WITNESSED
FOR CHRIST

Clarutza

AT THE TIME of my conversion there were small groups of
Christian Jews in Bucharest, Galatz, Jassy and other towns.
Among them were souls who had reached a very high spiritual
level.

In Bucharest, the Anglican Church Mission was active,
under the guidance of the Reverend J. Adenay, a clergyman
with a rare depth of faith and spirit of sacrifice.

Gradually the number of Christian Jews grew. The first
soul I won for the Lord was Clarutza, a young girl of about
sixteen. Her great-grandfather had been a Greek Orthodox
priest, who had been converted to Mosaic Judaism during a
movement of Judaisers which originated in the Ukraine at the
beginning of the last century. (A similar movement exists to
this day in Rumania among peasants who originally belonged
to a branch of the Adventists. Native Rumanian peasants are
circumcised and worship in the synagogues with a more burning
zeal than the Jews, many of whom, truth to say, show no
particular enthusiasm in carrying out their religious duties.)

This girl had been chosen by God to make good her great-
grandfather's error, by becoming a Christian. As soon as she
started attending our meetings, her parents began to persecute
her. They forbade her to meet with us. Then she decided
to start a hunger strike. She refused to eat until she was allowed
to go and visit her brethren in the faith. She fasted for three
days; on the fourth day, when her parents saw how weak she
had become, they told her she was free to go. "Not at all," she

answered. "I shall continue my hunger strike, and I shall not go until you come with me." After she had fasted for another day, her parents yielded on this point too, and from then on they regularly accompanied her to our meetings.

Clarutza was young in the faith; but I, her spiritual father, was also young in the faith. I, who had not yet been cured myself began to cure others. It was bound to have consequences.

One day, while she was having a meal at our house, she suddenly asked: "Brother, do you take a ticket in the lottery?" I had a ticket in my pocket, but for a long time I had been engaged in a spiritual struggle, because an inner voice had told me that God's children are not allowed to indulge in a game of chance—while at the same time the prospect of winning a large sum tempted me considerably. My conscience had not been appeased. Before I had time to consider, the answer came from my lips: "No", when I should have said "Yes". This was not the only lie I told at this time. Lying had become second nature to me, and even after I had been converted it played many tricks on me.

How I wished I could unsay the lie that had escaped my lips, but it was no longer possible. Never in my life have I regretted things I have not said, but I have often regretted words I have said. It is a good thing to keep the door locked, and not to let a word slip out. The man who does not take care to reduce the volume of his spoken words, has not been converted.

Pride, and maybe fear too, fear of undermining the confidence which this young girl had in me, prevented me from putting things right immediately. For a week afterwards I found it impossible to pray. When I knelt down to recite "Our Father", I seemed to hear a voice answering: "Liar".

It is said that when the Roman general Titus, who afterwards became Emperor, was besieging Jerusalem in the year A.D. 71, and starvation and plague broke out in the city, the rabbi Johanan ben Zacai, one of the Jewish leaders, broke through the lines and made his way to Titus's tent, where he knelt before the general and said: "Lord, spare this city, where there are so many women and innocent children!" Titus answered: "You are lying, old rabbi!"—"But what lie have I told?" the old man asked in astonishment. "The lie," answered Titus, "is the first word you said. You called me 'Lord'. If I am Lord, why do you not open the gates of the city and receive me with triumphal arches and flowers? If I am Lord, why do you not obey me?"

In the same way, the first word we offer in our prayers is a lie. We say "Father" to Him whose commandments we do not fulfil. We lie, although the Father offers us the truth.

In the anguish of my soul, I went to Tudor Popescu, who at that time was the "senior" believer among us in Rumania. He had once been an Orthodox priest, but like Luther he had had the courage to oppose his Church's hierarchy, and to preach the true gospel. For this reason he had been expelled from the Church. But thousands of believers followed him, and he was now a leading personality in Christian circles in Rumania. He was a sincere friend of Christian Jews, and he preached to the Jews with great blessing.

I told this old brother of my affliction, and asked him what I should do. I told him of my fear that if I confessed to the girl that I had lied to her—I who had planted the seed of the love of Christ in her—then perhaps she would lose her faith.

Tudor Popescu answered: "You are right to be afraid. The least sin a man commits may prove a stumbling-block to another soul, and condemn that soul to perdition. For this reason you must be more vigilant another time. Nevertheless, my advice is that you should simply confess to her that you have lied. If, as a consequence of this, the girl loses her faith, then this will show that she was not one of the chosen ones of the Lord. You, on the other hand, will continue in the way of the Lord, fulfilling His commandments."

This experience revealed to me how profitable it is for believers to confess their sins not only to God, but also to a wise brother, who can give them advice. The biblical word for confession is *exomologeo*, which means "to confess outwardly". It is not wise for us to wallow in our own sin, and allow it to remain within us until it chokes our spiritual life.

I called Clarutza to me; I placed her in a comfortable chair facing me, told her what had happened, and asked her humbly to forgive me. She listened earnestly, and said: "This time I shall forgive you, but you must not do it again."

Full of joy that the burden had fallen from me, I related this to all who were present at the meeting the following Sunday. Immediately, one after the other, Christian Jews stood up and confessed various lies, dishonesties, and thefts, and this confession proved a great blessing to us all.

If a believer from another nation had been present and heard all these confessions, he would have received a very poor impression of the moral standard of the Christian Jews—and he would have been right.

In judging the moral condition of Christian Jews, one should first consider what is its cause. The great Christian church communities, with their many faults, have one indisputable good—they educate men and women in the belief that Christ is the Saviour. If a longing for God is aroused in the average Rumanian, Frenchman or German, he should have no problem in finding the road that leads to God. It is quite natural for him to turn to Christ as the Saviour. It would not occur to him to have to make a choice between Christ, Krishna or Mohammed.

Those who have not had the advantage of being born of Christian parents are in an entirely different situation. When a longing for God is aroused in them, they are offered the way of their own religious tradition—Mosaic, Mohammedan, Buddhist or Hindu. If they hear the gospel, a large proportion of their spiritual energy must be employed in overcoming the old prejudices against Christianity and the love of the religion into which they were born. They must overcome great intellectual difficulties before they can accept what must appear sheer madness to the human mind and logic—that my sins have been atoned for by the death of a carpenter on a cross two thousand years ago; because this carpenter, who made glue and doors, and sold his goods, just as all carpenters do, was really God, incarnate in man. And what is more, those who believe in Him are regarded by God not as sinners who have been forgiven, but as though they had never sinned. In the sight of God they are regarded as though they had been as obedient to His commandments as Jesus Christ himself, says the Heidelberg Catechism.

Still more spiritual energy is wasted when a Jew becomes a Protestant, because no one Protestant speaks with sufficient authority, and you cannot therefore simply follow in his footsteps. From the pulpit and in their writings Protestants fight against other Protestants. What one says is contradicted by others. Thus a Jew inevitably wastes a great deal of his spiritual energy before he discovers the truth. People who are Christian by birth are saved a great deal of this trouble.

No man, however, has unlimited stores of spiritual energy. The more energy he spends on one thing, the less he has left for anything else. The consumption of spiritual energy which is required to liberate him from traditional emotions derived from the religion of his people, and to solve the intellectual difficulties that face him, is so great that little is left for the struggle on the moral front.

Anyone who reads the Epistles of Paul carefully will note that this was the situation among the converts in the first congregations. Even Paul himself, a great believer, complained about his thorn in the flesh.

The low moral standards of Christian Jews, of converts from other non-Christian religions and from atheism must be understood and accepted as an inevitable reality. The strong souls, those who have reached a high moral level—some because they have centuries of Christian influence behind them—must patiently and lovingly welcome the weaker brethren who are making their first steps on the new road of love. They belong to a race which for two thousand years has been separated from its Lord. Older Christians must not be frightened by the many and grievous lapses which the Jewish Christians suffer, nor by any relapse.

Clarutza gave us great joy.

Once she went with us to the summer resort of Sinaia. I went to call on the abbot of the monastery, and asked for permission to sell gospels and other Christian literature outside the church on Sunday morning. He was far too lazy to investigate whether our literature was Orthodox or not. The Greek Orthodox

Church, compared to the Roman Catholic Church, is like a village without any dogs. Its priests have fallen asleep. This allows great scope for evangelical work within its walls—occasionally, too, under the protection of its leaders, who take no interest in what is going on under their roof. So we set up a stall with Protestant literature right in front of the church entrance, where those who came to worship at this time of year belonged to the élite of Rumania, since Sinaia was the King's summer residence.

Our stall was surrounded by a great crowd. They were astonished, having never seen a gospel, because the Greek Orthodox Church does not place these books in the hands of believers. I had copies of St. John's Gospel, beautifully bound. Churchgoers, even monks, asked whether it had been written by John the Baptist, of whom they had heard. Clarutza stood by my side, and our books sold like hot cakes; we could hardly satisfy the demand.

On several occasions a police constable patrolled the fringe of the crowd. We looked like suspicious characters. It is a highly debatable point whether all criminals have typical character-istics, but at that time in Rumania one was justified in assuming that faces so typically Jewish obviously suggested that a crime was in the offing; and the two of us looked decidedly Jewish.

The police constable came nearer, and asked me politely what my name was. I answered him pointedly: "Richard Wurmbrand." He was somewhat taken aback, as it sounded German. It was a name I might well have borne in common with any of Hitler's supporters. He retired, with a salute.

A little further off he paused, and looked back at us. Our faces were hardly what he would have described as typically Aryan. He approached once again, and asked us to produce our identity cards. This was our undoing. At that time our identity cards specified our ethnic origins; and we were guilty of having the same ethnic origins as Jesus, whom the policeman, too, worshipped.

It is hard to describe the uproar that followed. He started to shout at the top of his voice: "These dirty Jews have desecrated our church and our gospel!" A crowd soon gathered. When the people inside the church heard the noise, they came out, and when they heard that the gospel had been desecrated by Jews they demanded their money back, as they refused to read anything written by a Jew. The hubbub increased. One Orthodox lady who knew us, had the courage to stand up in public and call out aloud to those who were standing on the church steps: "You should be ashamed of yourselves! Instead of rejoicing with Jews who belong to the same people as Jesus, who love Him, and give us His gospel, which our priests have not given us, you are picking a quarrel with these innocent people!" The others refused to listen to her; the abbot, to whom we had appealed, excused himself and vanished. The result was that we were arrested, and accused of the serious offence of daring to sell Christian literature, that is, gospels written by Jews, despite the fact that we were Jews.

We were taken to the police station. As it was Sunday morning there was only one officer there, and we were left in his charge. He told us that the police inspector would arrive and determine our fate, and handed us over to a third person, omitting to tell him that we were under arrest. The telephone rang, summoning him to the scene of a traffic accident, which left only Clarutza, myself, and a junior constable who did not know why we were there. I asked Clarutza: "Are you frightened?"—"Far from it," she replied. "I am enjoying myself. It is lovely to have an experience of this kind with Jesus." Calmly we awaited the arrival of the police inspector.

When he arrived, without asking the permission of the constable, I went up to him. I introduced myself, without mentioning that I was a Jew, or that I had been arrested. I told him: "I've come to sell religious literature in your town, and I want to ask your permission first." "Have you a permit from the Ministry of Culture?" he asked me. "No," I answered. "Then I'm afraid you cannot sell your literature," the inspector declared. I said: "Then I'll take my literature with me and go." "Very good," he said, instructing the constable accordingly.

Without waiting for him to say any more, we disappeared. We stopped the first taxi and left Sinaia. Later on, we had many a good laugh when we thought of the face the inspector must have made when he discovered that we had already sold our literature and had been under arrest.

Clarutza was baptised. Shortly after her baptism she emigrated with her parents to the Soviet Union, to escape from Fascism, which was then flourishing in Rumania. She wrote to us from Russia. Not long afterwards, the Fascists penetrated deep into Russian territory. The Rumanian brethren, who were of one mind and heart with us, went to look for her in the ghettoes that were set up by the Hitlerites. In answer to our prayer the Greek Orthodox Bishop Antim Nica and other monks went through the ghettoes, giving help to the Jews, an act of mercy that might well have cost them their lives. They found no trace of Clarutza.

Alba

Life had dragged Alba into the mire of sin. But Christ saved her while she was still a young girl, perhaps about twenty years old. Seldom have I met such an ardent soul as this daughter of Israel.

One day she came to see me, and said: "Brother, you cannot guess where I have been." I knew that she did unusual things, and I was prepared for anything. "Brother, I've been to see the renowned Rabbi X."

"What should you want of him?"

"I told him I was a great sinner, and asked him what I should do to be saved. He was not used to questions of this kind, but looked at me in astonishment over his glasses, and said: 'If up till now you have done many evil things, then from now on you must do good things.' I said: 'For the simple reason that God has given me this day as a gift, I owe it to Him to do as many good deeds as possible. But how can the good that I do today atone for the evil I did yesterday? This will not appease my conscience. What can I do?' The rabbi answered: 'The only thing I can tell you to do is to do good.' I then put this question to him: 'Is it not true that the blood shed by Jesus on the Cross cleanses me of my former sin?' The rabbi, who had grown suspicious, answered with another question: 'Is it not true that you have come from Wurmbrand?' 'Yes,' I answered, 'I have come from him. He preaches that the sacrifice which Jesus made on the Cross purifies us from all our sins, and I have come to ask you whether what he preaches is true.' Shaking his head, the rabbi replied: 'Beliefs differ. Some believe in Moses, others in Jesus, others in the Buddha or Mohammed. Everyone according to his wish.' 'No,' I answered, 'Jesus cannot be compared with any of the founders of other religions. It is written of Jesus in the Song of Solomon: "My beloved is the chiefest among ten thousand" (Song of Sol. 5.10). All honour to all the founders of the great religions: they are not Jesus's competitors. Jesus cannot be rivalled. The Scriptures call them the Saviour's companions, as in the Song of Solomon 1.7, but Jesus is unique among them.'"

Such was Alba.

She was always present at the street meetings which we held at that time, and which in Rumania were an entirely new and unusual phenomenon. She was tireless in the work of distributing gospels to Russian soldiers, and in front of the synagogues.

One of the pamphlets we distributed caused a considerable stir. It was called *The Meaning of the Easter Ritual*. On the Jewish Easter Eve a ritual is carried out by the master of the house in every household; this ritual is called *Afikoimen*. An evening meal is prepared, and everyone in the house, including guests, partakes of it. The meal is called *Seder*. During this meal the master of the house takes a dish containing three pieces of *matza* or unleavened bread, which up till then have been covered with a towel. A special prayer is said; the first piece of *matza* is placed to one side. The second piece is broken (in Poland it was customary to pierce it). The children are sent out of the room, and then the broken piece is hidden. The children return. All the grown-ups taking part in the meal have to drink three goblets of wine, but before the third goblet is drunk, the children are told to look for the hidden pieces of bread. When they find them, they are given presents, and cries of delight are uttered.

The pamphlet we distributed commented on this custom, and gave the explanation which we knew: the three pieces of bread represent the Father, the Son and the Holy Ghost; thus the second piece represents the second person of the Deity. The breaking of bread signifies the body of our Saviour broken on the Cross, the hiding signifies the burial. The three goblets represent the three days he had to spend in the tomb, and the rediscovery of the bread and the shouts of delight represent the joy of the Resurrection.

It was then explained that Israel had received prophecies foretelling the Messiah, both in writings and in symbolical acts. *Afikoimen* is a symbolical act which has survived from the pre-Christian era. Owing to their religious conservatism, the religious Jews continue to practise it, but it is now an empty husk, stripped of its contents. The Jews carry out this ritual act without realising that it symbolises the sufferings and resurrection of the Saviour. The pamphlet concluded with a request to anyone who had a better explanation to let us have it.

Our pamphlets had a very attractive appearance. On the outside was printed: *Jewish Religious Library*. If we had put *Christian Library*, no Jew would have read them. The cover was in the national colours of the Jews, white and blue, with the Star of David.

Alba and the other brethren and sisters sold great quantities of this pamphlet on the Eve of the Passover in front of the synagogues.

The Jewish community and the Zionist papers, which reviled me in practically every edition, fumed with rage, but in a way that was very gratifying to us, for under the heading "A New Lie from Pastor Wurmbrand" they repeated the essential points of our argument, and in this way those Jews who had not read our booklet learned what it contained. After the text had been reproduced, there followed such words of abuse as "traitor", "mercenary lackey", "disgusting" and so on, words which also convinced us of the need to examine ourselves spiritually, and provided a serious warning from God that we should beware of treading the slippery path to which these terms of abuse might lead.

Alba could not bear the thought that her elder brother hould be insulted. Without a word to us, she went to the editor of the newspaper and asked to speak to the author of the article attacking me.

She told him: "I have read your article, and I should like to know what is the real interpretation of the *Afikoimen* ritual.

"It is not the interpretation given by that traitor Wurmbrand."

"So I understand from your article. I should now like to ask you respectfully if you could give me the true interpretation."

"It is quite different from the one which that disgusting Wurmbrand has given."

"Would you be so kind as to tell me what it is?"

"Mr. Wurmbrand is a man who has sold himself."

"That may be so, but what is the true interpretation of the ritual?"

Neither he nor anyone else could disprove our statements, neither in this respect nor in any others. All that remained was their abuse.

At night Alba and the others fixed posters on the walls of houses and on fences, calling on the Jews to be converted. During the cold winter nights placards were posted, bearing the title: "Christmas—the National Holiday of the Jews". The text underneath stated that every nation gladly celebrates the birthday of its great men, of whom they are proud. It was at Christmas that the greatest man, He who is celebrated and worshipped by all peoples, was born to the Jewish people. Everyone honours the greatest Jew, only the Jews remain indifferent to Him who is called in the Bible "The glory of His people Israel". The posters advised the Jews once again to relent, and to rejoice with other peoples at the Christmas festival.

We were now the target of a new and furious attack.

A Zionist paper wrote: "Mr. Wurmbrand wishes to introduce Christmas and other Christian customs among the Jews. As he is very importunate, it is possible that he might finally convince us. We shall adopt the various customs, including that of *coliva* (a cake which is distributed at funerals in the Greek Orthodox Church). And the first *coliva* we shall eat will be at Mr. Wurmbrand's funeral."

This was a threat of death.

Alba lived by our side: she shared with us in all our struggles, all our dangers, and in all our battles she was in the front line.

A poor alcoholic, a profoundly religious man, asked me to heal him of his affliction. At that time I was still ignorant of the technique of healing alcoholics by faith, which is very simple. I was unsuccessful. But Alba would not give up. She went to visit him in the tavern, where he was sitting in a drunken stupor, and talked to him until he was converted and was healed. He has since converted other souls to the faith, and these again have converted others.

Let me at this point make a few general observations.

People with a burning desire to carry out missionary work are apt to hurt the feelings of Jews, often causing a violent reaction. It has been questioned whether this kind of missionary work can be right. Even Jesus warned against proselytising when He said: "Woe unto you, scribes and Pharisees, hypocrites! For ye compass sea and land to make one proselyte, and when he is made, ye make him twofold more the child of hell than yourselves" (Matt. 23.15).

But all these considerations, both for and against, cannot prevent people like Alba from being what they are at a particular stage in their development. Lamartine wrote:

> *Je chantais, mes amis, comme l'homme respire,*
> *comme l'oiseau gémit, comme le vent soupire*
> *comme l'eau murmure en coulant.*
> I sang, my friends, as a man breathes,
> As the bird laments, as the wind sighs,
> As the water murmurs when it flows.

The many Albas of this world speak about Jesus because it is their nature to do so; no argument can make me stop breathing; no argument can prevent those who love Jesus from witnessing for Him, just as no argument can prevent some people reacting violently to their witness instead of taking it calmly.

There are many different psychological types among human beings; the extrovert, when he is converted, becomes a missionary, the introvert becomes a contemplative. God's law is one: "Therefore all things whatsoever ye would that men should do to you, do ye even so to them" (Matt. 7.12). With all my heart I long that any man who is convinced that he possesses a truth which can make me blessed here and in eternity should spare no effort to tell it to me. We consider as normal compulsory schooling, compulsory vaccination, forcing a child to eat something good, even though he may not appreciate it. Why then should we consider missionary activity as morally unjustified? I am grateful to old Wölfkes because he showed me the way, and it is my conviction that the children of God ought to exercise their missionary activity likewise.

We, too, say to Jesus the words which Abner, the captain of the host, once said to David: "I will arise and go, and will gather all Israel unto my lord the king, that they may make a league with thee, and that thou mayest reign over all that thine heart desireth" (2 Sam. 3.21).

The memory of Alba reminds me of something else: we must have patience with a soul. Alba grew in grace from day to day.

In Leviticus we read that whoever touches the carcase of an unclean animal shall wash his clothes—and be unclean until the evening (11.25). Even after you have washed your clothes, you are still unclean for a while. The salvation which Jesus gives is like medicine: one must wait a little while after taking it before feeling its effect. With some people it is necessary to wait longer than with others. The seed that falls on good ground brings forth good fruit; but we sow in spring and gather the fruit in autumn. However good the soil may be, it is impossible to harvest as soon as we have sown. Some trees produce fruit only after several years.

During the period of growth we must be grateful for the small fruits these souls produce, or for the future fruit that is still developing. The whole intention of Leviticus Chapter 5 is to teach us that, if we cannot offer the Lord as much as we should like to, we must offer whatever we can, at every stage of our development. All categories of believers have the same chances of finding favour with God.

New-born babies are usually ugly. A new-born soul who appears beautiful is probably striking a pose.

Alba not only overcame against sin, but in time she also wore the garment of great virtue. Those who were like her learned to understand a legend about Jesus which I often made use of in my sermons.

It is said that Jesus sent a message to one of his disciples, telling him that He would visit him together with His apostles. The man who received the message was very glad, and said to his son, who also loved the Saviour: "I shall make my house ready, and you must tidy the garden, so that the Lord will find it clean and swept."

The boy set to work energetically, sweeping and watering the garden. When everything was ready, his father came to see how his son had carried out his orders. He said to him: "Well done, my dear son. I can see that you have worked with great zeal. You have made the garden beautiful and tidy, but it is not tidy enough for the Lord. Work at it a little more."

The boy, who felt that this was a reproach, tidied up the garden once more. This time he gathered up every withered leaf, spruced up every drooping flower, and did all he possibly could to remove the least traces of disorder.

Once again his father inspected his work, and this time he said: "Very good; now it is really tidy, but it is still not tidy enough for the Lord."

The boy, who did not know what else he could do, asked: "But how does one make a garden neat for the Lord?"

His father's answer was: "If you work for His sake, it is not sufficient that you should remove all untidiness from the garden—you must also decorate it with everything that is beautiful, and which has not been grown in it so far. Go to the neighbours, and see if you can find some new plants that you can put in the ground; hang up beautiful carpets, and light lanterns. That is the way to make everything pleasant for the Lord."

This is precisely what Alba did.

It was her privilege to trace me to the prison where I was being secretly held under an assumed name, and she was the first to tell my family that I was still alive.

I did not see her for many years. Before I was released from prison, she left for Israel. But after coming to the West, I met her again, the same faithful, loving woman.

Mircea Petrescu

One day, Alba was sitting on a bus; opposite her was a man who, judging by his appearance, was an Orthodox Jew. She was filled with the desire to speak to him of Jesus.

We never missed an opportunity on the bus, in the market-place, on the street, wherever occasion offered.

The thought that all people could become like Jesus, but that they do not know this and die in affliction; the thought that man is second in rank after God Himself (angels are the ministering spirits of mankind), and that he nevertheless lives without being aware of the truth, made us weep. Our prayer meetings were harrowing, and many tears were shed.

My suffering became unbearable; when I walked in the streets it was like a stab in my heart every time someone passed by and the question arose: "I wonder if he has been saved?" One of our sisters in the faith, who is now dead, always had tears in her eyes when she thought of the eternal fate that awaited the people she met in the street. I prayed God to take this suffering from me, or I should not be able to live, and the Lord heard my prayer.

Alba did not weep; she always smiled her winning smile, a smile which had the same source as my suffering. She said to herself: "Since bad girls attract men with their smiles, why should I not use my smile to convert men to good?"

But however would she be able to get into conversation with this Orthodox Jew? These men are serious, sober citizens, not in the habit of opening up a conversation with an unknown woman. It is written in the *Pirkei Abot*, the Teachings of the Parents, in the Babylonian Talmud: "Do not speak to a woman." The rabbis say: "This refers to one's own woman—how much more to another's woman!" For this reason the wise men said: "As often as a man speaks to a woman, it shall be his misfortune."

Alba therefore decided to sing a song in the crowded bus.

The message of her song, she hoped, would go straight to the heart of the Jew.

To her amazement the man asked her: "What sort of song is that?" She answered his question, and told him about the Saviour who had given His life on the Cross. He listened to her with the closest attention, and finally expressed a wish to hear more about our faith. She asked him to leave the bus with her, and to accompany her to my house.

And so it came about that they both walked in through my door.

When the Jew introduced himself, I expected to hear a Jewish name, but instead I heard a rattling good Rumanian one. And the story he told me was a strange one.

Despite his highly Jewish appearance, he was not a Jew, but a Rumanian who had been converted to Judaism and had adopted Jewish dress and all Jewish customs.

This man, who was a talented painter, told me how it had happened. While he was still a small boy, he was incensed when he saw Christian children hitting Jewish children. He defended the Jews, and his reward was that he was persecuted together with them.

When the war broke out and he realised that it was not a question of defending his fatherland only, but of committing crimes and sacrilege by murdering innocent Jews who were killed in their hundreds of thousands together with their women and children, he deserted from the front, at the risk of his life. He would rather die than be a murderer. He loved the victims of this cruel and senseless persecution, and he asked himself: "If Jesus were in Rumania now, whose side would He be on: on the side of the Jews or of the Christians who kill Jews?" There could only be one answer to this question: on the side of the victims.

The Pharisees, who hated Jesus with a violent and profound hatred, remembered vividly His burning love for Israel, how He once said: "Salvation is of the Jews" (John 4.22). This clearly emerges in a fantastic and unattractive, but highly significant, story in the Talmud, the holy book of the Pharisees.

In the *Gittim* we read of Onkelos bar Kalinikos, a grandchild

of the Roman emperor Titus, the man who destroyed Jerusalem.
This young man wished to adopt the Jewish religion. But before
he did so he summoned the spirit of Titus, and asked him:
"Which people is most highly thought of in the other world?"
"Israel," answered Titus. "Shall I join them?" Titus replied
that they had too many rules and regulations, which cannot
be fulfilled. "It would be better if you persecuted them, for
then you would be great. For it is written in the Book of
Lamentations that 'her [Israel's] children are gone into captivity before the enemy'" (Lam. 1.5). Titus was then asked
what his punishment was, and he said that he had brought his
punishment down upon his own head: every day his ashes
were gathered together, he was brought to life, he was condemned, he was burned again, and his ashes spread over the
seven seas.

After this Onkelos summoned Balaam, the false prophet,
and asked him: "Which people is most highly thought of in the
other world?" "Israel," answered Balaam. "Shall I join them?"
Balaam answered: "You must not seek their fortune or their
prosperity eternally all your days." Then Onkelos asked him
what his punishment was, and Balaam replied that he had
boiling filth poured over him. (As Balaam had failed to carry
out the command of Balak, King of the Moabites, to curse the
Jews, he advised the Midianites, who were the neighbours of
the Moabites, to send their daughters into the Jewish camp,
in order to lead the Jews into sin, and in that way bring down
the wrath of the Lord upon them. Hence this punishment.)
Then Onkelos summoned the spirit of Jesus (this name occurs
only in the old editions of the Talmud, which were not censored
by the Inquisition. The censored editions, instead of using the
name Jesus, have inserted the phrase *Poshe Israel*, the Sinner
of Israel) and asked Him: "Which people is most highly
thought of in the other world?" Jesus answered: "Israel."
"Shall I join them?" Jesus answered: "You must seek to
promote the best interests of Israel and not its destruction.
To destroy Israel is to destroy the light of God's eyes."

Even Jesus's bitterest enemies repeat the undeniable fact
that Jesus loved Israel.

Petrescu loved Jesus: for this reason it was natural for him to side with the Jews, against anti-Semitic Christians.

Only that human soul who receives no help from the grace of God cannot abide by the golden mean, but lapses into extremes. Petrescu was right to deny a false Christianity, a Christianity full of hatred. But in denying it, we must also realise the secret of the great decline of the Church, the Church that Jesus had promised He would be with all its days.

In Matthew's Gospel, after the account of the healing of many who were sick and possessed of devils, we are told that in this way Jesus "Himself took our infirmities, and bare our sicknesses" (Matt. 8.17). (The literal translation is: He assumed our weaknesses.)

When Christ was made man, He subjected Himself to all the circumstances of life; He could exert His influence through the Word, but He was also able to be moved by others. He healed thousands of their sins, and destroyed the hatred with which thousands of others were consumed. But the sin and hatred which He took away from others fell on Him. All the weaknesses which people have taken with them into church, all the sins which Christians have committed for two thousand years, have become His weaknesses, His powerlessness. A refusal on His part to accept the weak would mean lack of love; to receive them would mean that He assumed the shame of their weakness and sin—it meant in fact allowing the crimes of Christians to fall upon His head.

Leviticus contains the phrase "all these abominations" (Lev. 18.27). The word for "these" is *Eleh;* but the text actually contains what no translator has dared to translate, *toevot ha-El,* which means nothing less than—*horribile dictu*—"God's abominations". The serious thing about any abomination committed by someone who worships God, is precisely that it redounds to the Holy Name, and in the eyes of men it passes for an abomination of God. And is it not so that people judge God unjustly for the injustices which they, who pass for His worshippers, commit?

A Latin proverb says: *Qui bene distinguet, bene docet,* which means, "He who distinguishes well, teaches well".

Sins are only reflected back on Jesus—they are associated with His name, He bears them, but He is innocent. Nobody should reject Christ because of crimes committed by Christians.

In this respect the Jews created confusion in the sentimental heart of our artist friend. A Kabalistic rabbi caught him in his net, and persuaded him to abandon the Christian faith, and adopt the Mosaic. We endeavour to turn Jews into Christians; he had been converted from Christianity to Judaism.

The struggle was a difficult one, because we were dealing with an idealist, and a person with high moral standards. It is always difficult to convert someone who knows himself to be a decent person. Step by step, I showed him the prayers of the synagogue, and asked him if he accepted them, because—credulous as he had been—he had been made to say them while at the same time he had failed to realise that in entering the synagogue he had made a clean break with the Jesus who had taught him to be good and to love.

Every morning the Jews say: "Blessed art Thou, Jehovah, King of the World, because Thou hast not made me a 'goy' (gentile), a slave or a woman." I asked him: "Do you accept the belief that you are an inferior creature, lower than every Jew, merely because you were born a Rumanian? What else is this but racial prejudice? At the Feast of the Passover the Jews stand up to pray to God: '*Shfoh hamotha al hagoim asher lo iediuha*, that is to say, 'Pour out Thy wrath over the peoples that do not know Thee!' Do you agree with a prayer of this kind? Is not Jesus's advice to His apostles superior, to go to all people and preach the gospel, and in this way teach them how to escape the wrath of God and to start a new life in love?"

I also showed him the inconsistencies of the Jewish prayer book. There were prayers used in the ritual on the great Day of Atonement which had been inserted by Jews who believed secretly in Jesus. They ask God that these prayers may be received "*al-iad Jeshu Metatron*"—through Jesus standing before the Throne. *Metatron* is the Kabalistic name for the Messiah.

On the same day another prayer is offered up, which has

not yet been translated in any of the vernacular editions of the Hebrew prayer books. This starts with the words "*Az milifnei beresit*". The rabbis have good grounds for leaving this prayer untranslated, because it says: "The Messiah, our justification, has forsaken us. We are defeated, and there is no one to bring us justice. He has been killed and pierced for our sins. We have been healed by His wounds. The time for the victory of the new creation is at hand. He ascendeth on high in a chariot. He shines forth from Seir to hear us for a second time on the mountains of Lebanon."

It is obvious that He who has been pierced for our sins, in order that we should have forgiveness, can be none other than Jesus. The synagogue sings hymns of adoration to Him, although it rejects Him, in the same way as some priests, while singing of repentance in every liturgy, are furious if anyone mentions repentance to them.

Gradually a light dawned in Petrescu's heart. He realised that the Mosaic religion is of necessity a false religion, because it is an autosoteric religion, that is to say, a religion in which one's salvation depends on one's own exertions. Autosoterism is lack of humility; neither sin nor salvation comes from us. Men's fates have been determined a long time ago, and from a long way away, and eternal life is a gift of God, just as sin comes from Satan and is not an act of free will.

One Christmas Eve, when the candles were lit, Petrescu said calmly: "Today, Jesus has been born in me, too."

Petrescu is unique: he is a pure Rumanian, and at the same time a Christian Jew, seeing that he has come to Christianity from Judaism. Later he also became chairman of the board of trustees in our church. He is still a steadfast brother and a faithful friend. He is married to a Christian Jewess.

One day I was preparing my sermon in a park; I was reading the Bible, and a young girl beside me was also reading a book. I tried to see what it was. It was a novel by a Rumanian author. I said to her: "I have read your book, but do you know my book?" Thus started a conversation which ended with the young lady's conversion—and subsequently that of her mother. I baptised the mother at the height of a violent bombing attack. The girl is now married to Petrescu, and they are living happily together.

Spurgeon says that when God closed the gates of Paradise, He did not entirely close them; He left a small corner of it, a truly Christian marriage. Their home is a corner of Paradise just like that.

Holy Moishe

Let others praise their great intellectuals: I should like to praise the fool whom God chose to shame the wise.

Our brother Moishe was by trade a pall-bearer at funerals; he suffered from a gentle form of madness, which was not dangerous to others. At our meetings he would weep copiously, and make an awful din when the preacher spoke of our Saviour's sufferings, and laughed aloud when he spoke of His victory.

The other believers in the congregation considered Moishe a disturbing element. One of them promised him—he was very poor—that if he would only keep quiet during the services, he could come and dine at his house every Sunday, and enjoy roast meat, cakes and fruit.

For one whole Sunday Moishe kept comparatively calm; but the following week, when the preacher spoke of the Resurrection, he stood up in the middle of the sermon and shouted: "Roast or no roast, hallelujah!"

In 1939 an anti-Semite fired a shot at the Chief Rabbi Niemerover. The intended victim was not hurt, the bullet passing through his overcoat, but the excitement made him ill, and he was forced to stay in bed. A great many Jews called to congratulate him on his lucky escape. Among these was Moishe. He said to the rabbi: "Don't you see, Your Eminence, that God does not want sinners to die, but He wants them to be converted and saved?"

He came to our house to dinner, and as we were about to start he said to my wife: "Sister, will you please remove my knife. I know that I am mad, and I have promised God never to touch a knife, lest in an unguarded moment I should injure someone. After all, Adam and Eve ate without using knives."

I reflected that a great many wise men had a lot to learn from this madman.

In January 1940, a revolt took place in Bucharest led by the Legion of the Archangel Michael, a Fascist organisation. A great many Jews were killed; some of them were flayed, and suspended on hooks in the slaughterhouse under the inscription "Kosher Meat".

Moishe was sitting in a cheap teahouse when a gang of Fascists burst in. Their leader shouted: "All dirty Jews clear out!" The Jews went outside, where they were herded into lorries, to be driven to the woods and shot. Moishe, who was easily recognisable as a Jew, sat quietly drinking his tea. The leader of the greenshirts shouted at him: "You dirty Jew, didn't you hear me? I told you to get out!" Moishe answered calmly: "Dear brother, dirty Jews are those who do what Judas did—he sold Jesus. I am an Israelite who loves our Saviour."—"Shut up and get outside!" So Moishe went outside. The order rang out: "Into the lorry, you dirty Jew!" Moishe repeated what he had said: "Dirty Jews are those who do what Judas did—they sell Jesus. I am an Israelite who loves Him." One of the leaders of the gang exclaimed: "Leave him alone. You can see that he is a preacher." And they left him in peace.

But Moishe, instead of departing, said to the man: "I can see that you are good and merciful. God will reward you for this. But don't stop at half measures; let the other Jews in the lorry go home, too." Mad people often possess tremendous powers of suggestion, and I believe that Moishe had this power, but from another source. At any rate, the greenshirt ordered the other Jews out of the lorry, and allowed them to go home.

Now Moishe was thoroughly scared; he went home and remained in hiding throughout the time that the pogrom lasted.

All the Jews he had saved told this story of Moishe to everyone they met, and because he had vanished, and was believed to be dead, he was referred to as "Holy Moishe".

He later suffered a tragic fate, dying of jaundice in a concentration camp.

Bertha

Christian missions have often been reproached for giving material help to poor Jews, and in this way buying souls.

This is a difficult problem.

Many of the Jews lived in poverty, and our work was directed especially to assisting these needy persons. How could we avoid helping them materially? How could we avoid helping Jewish refugees out of Hitler's Germany? It is written that Jesus had compassion on the multitude. This compassion is also a characteristic of His true followers. Jesus had compassion on men and women because they were hungry, not only because they were not saved. He was concerned with the problem of feeding them. If we help a person and at the same time preach the gospel to him, these two things will be associated in the minds of onlookers, and of those who obtain relief. Jesus encountered the same difficulty. He preached the new teaching, but at the same time He gave bread to the poor and hungry. The result of this was that many people came to Him only to receive loaves and fishes, which He also gave them.

There is a very old Jewish legend about Abraham. One day he invited a beggar into his tent. He wished to show him hospitality and prepared a meal for him. But when he said grace, the beggar began to curse God, declaring that he could not bear to hear His name. The pious Abraham drove the beggar away; he could not stand hearing anyone cursing his heavenly Friend in his own tent. But God appeared to him, and said: "This man has cursed me and reviled me for fifty years, and yet I give him food to eat every day, and could you not show him hospitality for one single day? You might at any rate have waited to drive him out until after he had eaten."

If we must feed those who curse God, how much more those who pretend they are worshipping Him! Also, it is very difficult to be certain whether a man is pretending, or whether he is really a believer.

In Jesus's well-known parable the prodigal son returned to his father for material reasons, and yet he was received with the greatest love.

Truth is weak; it has never triumphed unless it has been able to offer material advantages, unless it has dressed itself in beautiful apparel, and unless it has been able to make an appeal to the emotions.

Old Simeon said of Jesus: "This child is set for the fall and rising again of many in Israel" (Luke 2.34), in other words not only for raising up but also for a fall.

Some Jews who were shown Christian charity in the form of material assistance, were thereby raised to unexpected heights of belief. Such was Bertha.

One might say of Bertha what Disraeli once said when he was reproached for having married for money: "Yes, when I married I knew so little about my wife that I would not have taken her without her money. But now that I know her so well, I would be willing to marry her even if she were poor."

Other Jews, on the other hand, have suffered a disastrous fall as a result of material help, which brought a corruption to their souls from which they have never been able to recover.

A certain sculptor who was profoundly moved by stories of the first Christian martyrs had made up his mind to create works of art which would immortalise the Christians who had been thrown to the wild beasts. He sculpted a young man and a young woman—the man holding a cross in his hand—and then started to work on a lion, crouched ready to hurl himself at the two figures.

One day he called his friends to his studio to show them his work. The lion was still only an unshaped lump of clay.

One of his friends said: "You are a poor man. How can you sell this work? There are many artists who make sculptures like this, and no Jew would buy a work of art with a cross in it. Remove the cross, and replace it with a key. The key is a holy symbol in many religions. It might remind you of the keys of St. Peter, but it is also a holy symbol for spiritualists and other occultists. This will make it easier for you to find a buyer."

And so the sculptor changed the cross into a key.

Then a wealthy American walked into his studio and exclaimed: "What a magnificent work of art! It symbolises thrift. The little lump of clay might represent a money-safe, and the young man with the key teaches people to be thrifty in spending their money. I will give you a thousand dollars for this work."

In this way a sculpture which was originally intended to extol martyrdom was transformed into a work in honour of money.

There are many souls who are inspired at first with the love of Jesus, but as they are poor and receive material aid, the picture of the Master is gradually blotted out. What really concerns them is how much help they can get, and where they can get it, and above all, whether anyone else has received more than they have.

But this only happens to some.

Bertha openly confessed that, to start with, she came to us because she was attracted by the rumour that we helped poor Jews. But after she believed in Jesus with all her heart, she never again appealed to us for help, although she was very poor.

She was married to a German citizen, who was half-Jewish. He was not converted. They had three sons. In 1943 the German legation in Rumania published an order to the effect that all German citizens were to be repatriated. She stayed behind in Rumania. He and their three children, who according to the racial thinking at that time suffered the great tragedy of being three-quarters Jewish, made their way to Germany.

In Germany an informer revealed that the husband was not only half-Jewish, but was even married to a Jewess, and that his children therefore had mostly Jewish blood in their veins, and only a drop of Siegfried's blood.

They were all imprisoned by the Gestapo, and over their head hung the threat of the death camp. In order to save his life, the man told a lie, declaring that his wife was Rumanian. The German police offered him the chance of writing home to ask the authorities to forward documents to show that his wife was of Aryan extraction. If this could be proved, the children would be three-quarters Aryan, and they would be saved.

In those days in Rumania, everything could be arranged with the help of money. Bertha's family obtained papers showing she was of pure Aryan blood—more Aryan than Hitler, whose origins, according to rumour, were a little mixed.

I was in her home when her relatives brought her the false documents which would save her husband and three children from the gas chambers of Auschwitz, and I witnessed a scene which I shall remember to my dying day. She tore the false documents to pieces and declared: "Abraham was willing to sacrifice one child to God; I shall sacrifice three children and a husband, but I refuse to tell a lie!"

She had no further news of her husband and children.

Meister Eckhardt wrote that he who leaves behind things in the form in which they exist—empty, haphazard—will receive them back in their pure essence, in the eternal essence. He who leaves things in their lowest form, in which they are mortal, will receive them back from God in their true form. Bertha will have her family restored to her in glory.

Bertha will never know how magnificent was her gesture: she is a humble sister. The brethren do not know of her sacrifice, because she has not breathed a word of it to them. And, what is more, when she discussed with the brethren the case of someone who had obtained false documents in order to escape persecution, she declared: "Let us not judge him! Every man must follow his own conscience."

Did Bertha do right or wrong? She judges no one, and in this way she is raised above the judgement of men.

This raises the question of whether we should always speak the truth.

Christian writings from the fourth century record the lives and meditations of the first generations of monks. These monks lived in the desert of the Thebaid, where they had fled from the corruption which entered the Church when Christianity became the recognised religion. In this book we read that one day Father Agathon asked Father Alonie: "How shall I contrive to keep my tongue from telling lies?" The answer was: "If you do not lie you will commit many sins." So he asked him: "How is this possible?" And he answered: "Lo, two men have committed a murder before your eyes, and one of them has taken refuge in your cell. Then comes the judge, seeking him, and he asks you: 'Was a murder committed before your eyes?' If you do not lie you will condemn a man to death. It is better that you should let him be judged by God, since He knows everything."

Luther says that to lie to protect someone else or in jest is not a lie. For myself, I believe that there is a confusion between the concept of a lie and an untruth. *Faust*, *Othello* and *Parsifal* are not the truth, but neither are they lies; they are art. The fairy stories we tell our children, or the jokes we tell grown-ups to amuse them, are not lies. They belong to an entirely different sphere, the realm of fantasy and play. Is it a lie to tell an untruth in order to save the life, honour or property of an innocent person who is being hounded by an executioner who persecutes truth and purity? Should we give such an unpleasant name to an action which springs from love?

A lie is the untruth I speak in order to injure my neighbour. "Love and do what you will," says Augustine. Is good better than truth; and an untruth that saves a life is better than a truth that destroys it. In the dictatorial, anti-Christian countries, this is an everyday and acute problem for believers.

But what about Abraham's sacrifice of Isaac? There is a sphere of sanctity where our practical judgements lose their power.

I wonder if truth could have survived in the many labyrinths of life if, here and there, there had not lived anonymous heroes of the calibre of Bertha, who sacrificed all they held dear for the sake of truth? I have often heard superficial sermons, in which the preacher asked: "What would you lose if you became a Christian? Only the brandy bottle, your clothes, the stick with which you beat your wife, your name and reputation, your bad conscience, or the hell that exists in your home!" No, there are people who for the sake of their Christian conviction are prepared to lose their fortune, their freedom, their health, and even the persons they love most on earth!

A witness in our family

My wife comes from an orthodox Jewish family. After she was converted, she was unable to sleep at night for the thought of her parents, who were pious Jews. We travelled to Cernauti in order to talk to them, and we arrived on Friday evening, the start of the Jewish Sabbath.

The table was set for the ritual feast; the candles had been lit. The three sisters, who were younger than my wife, and my little brother-in-law who was only eight years old, looked at us respectfully. The parents' delight was unbounded; after all, I was the husband of their eldest daughter.

My father-in-law rose to his feet and recited the *Kidush*, the blessing of the wine. He was very surprised when he noticed me—whom he knew to be an atheist—joining in singing the old prayer based on Genesis 2.1–3: "Thus the heavens and the earth were finished, and all the host of them. And on the seventh day God ended his work which he had made; and he rested on the seventh day from all his work which he had made. And God blessed the seventh day, and sanctified it: because that in it he had rested from all his work which God created and made. Blessed art Thou, Jehovah, King of the World, that hast created the fruit of the vine."

After this, the bread was blessed, and the meal started. When it was over, and only the candles cast their shadows on the walls, I began to say: "It is written that God completed His work on the seventh day; and it is written again that on the seventh day God rested. What was it that was not perfect in all that had been created in the six days? What did God complete on the seventh? How did He complete it while He was resting?

"What He created in six days was not complete. Man still needed one thing: rest. God created this on the seventh day, and in this way He filled His world with His own rest.

"The Law of Moses may be compared to the first six days of the Creation. The Law contains six hundred and thirteen commandments, which do not give us rest, but which torment our conscience. We are constantly transgressing the Law. Who can maintain that he has kept at least two commandments: to love God with all his heart and all his soul and all his might and to love his neighbour as himself? The Law cannot be kept. It is only a mirror in which we see our own sinfulness, and how impossible it is for us as human beings to live apart from God, the God whose laws are just and holy and which have become a burden which we, sinners, cannot bear.

"In the old days the Jews could not be saved by keeping the Law—all the great men in the Bible describe how they themselves have often transgressed it—but by the sacrifice of atonement which was made in the temple. There was no forgiveness of sins without bloodshed. Sin was transferred, by the laying on of hands, to an innocent animal which symbolically represented the sacrifice which the future Messiah would make by His death for the sins of man. By slaughtering the animal the Jews appeased their conscience; it was brought as a sacrifice for their transgressions of the Law. But now we have neither a temple nor a sacrifice. How, then, can we be saved?"

My father-in-law answered: "The rabbis have taught us that if we recite daily a chapter of the Law of Moses dealing with sacrifice, God will count this as though we ourselves had made the sacrifice.

I answered: "I know that. One day a Christian walked into the shop of a very orthodox Jew, and started to talk to him on the subject we have just been discussing, the sacrifice, and he got the same answer as you have given me. This man did not continue the argument, but said: 'Every man should hold to his own convictions. I have not come here to discuss religion, but to buy goods.' And he asked for three shirts, six pairs of socks, a dozen handkerchiefs, and various other articles. Finally he asked the shopkeeper to give him a bill specifying all that he had purchased. The shopkeeper, who was delighted to have done such good business, wrote out a bill, and wrapped the purchases. The Christian read the bill aloud, took the parcel in his hand, and walked out of the shop.

The shopkeeper called after him: 'You have forgotten to pay!' The customer answered: 'Didn't I read the bill to you?' 'Yes, but you never paid.' To which the customer replied: 'Is'nt reading the bill the same as paying it?'

"If we reduce this to its purely practical meaning, we may say that the merchant was not satisfied with precisely the same approach as he used in his religion. The sacrifice must be made; reading about it is not enough."

I spoke with my father-in-law about the Messianic prophecies, which were fulfilled in Jesus. But acts speak more eloquently than verses in the Bible. The Jews are God's chosen people, chosen to bring the Light of God into the world. Millions of people who in ancient times worshipped Zeus, Jupiter, Wotan or other idols, today worship the true God, and regard the books written by our great prophets as their holy book. Who has raised the nations out of polytheism, and converted them to the worship of the only just, good God, the God of Israel, who demands a moral life? Jesus! Through Him the Messianic vocation with which our people had been entrusted was fufilled. Through Jesus's sufferings, crucifixion, and resurrection on the third day, through His life and death as a servant of God, through His existence as a man of suffering, as Isaiah had foretold, He has caused mankind to give their hearts to our God, and caused those who believed in a Saviour who died and rose again, whether they called him Adonis, Osiris, Dionysus or Heracles, to know the fulfilment in history of these ancient myths.

Jesus is the King of the Jews, the Messiah of Israel.

I told the children a great many other stories, and they listened to me with the deepest respect. My father-in-law became pensive. That evening my mother-in-law knelt in prayer with us.

The children began attending Christian meetings regularly; not long afterwards they embraced the faith. The old man was ashamed of being seen at a meeting, but as the time to go came nearer, he would call out in a loud voice that re-echoed through the house: "Hurry, hurry! Everyone gets there in time; my daughters are the only ones who are late!"

My little brother-in-law, who was receiving religious instruction from a great rabbi, resisted stubbornly. I have often been forced to wonder at the independence of thought and action shown by Jewish children when they are small. They are living examples of Blaise Pascal's remark: "Man is born as an original, and dies as a copy."

Converting anti-Semites

The community of Christian Jews was the very place where a great many anti-Semitic persons found Christ, during the period when Nazism reigned.

One anti-Semite who attended our church took part in the ill-treatment of a number of Jews on his way to a meeting; he had not been told by the person who had invited him that a Jew was going to preach. He became converted that very Sunday. He has never since that day struck a Jew.

Once, when a Rumanian sister brought another anti-Semite to our meeting, I preached a sermon based on Jesus's saying: "I am not sent but to the lost sheep of the house of Israel." (Matt. 15.24). It was a sermon meant to call the Jews to conversion; so I quoted biblical texts which aimed to prove that the gospel is first and foremost a message addressed to the Jews: "Go not into the way of the Gentiles, and into any city of the Samaritans enter ye not: but go rather to the lost sheep of the house of Israel" (Matt. 10.5–6) "Repentance and remission of sins should be preached in his name among all nations, beginning at Jerusalem" (Luke 24.47). "The gospel of Christ . . . is the power of God unto salvation to every one that believeth; to the Jew first, and also to the Greek" (Rom. 1.16).

When the meeting was over, the sister reproached me bitterly: "You know very well that we often bring to our meetings people who are not Jews, and who usually hate you. Why do you preach like that? The Rumanians would be offended by your sermons, which are too pro-Jewish."

Our anti-Semitic friend went home after the meeting, and argued to himself as follows: "Did you hear what the Bible says? The Jew first, and then the other nations. But where does the hater of the Jews come in? Nowhere." He gave up his anti-Semitism, as well as his other sins, and was converted. He became an enthusiastic fisher of men, and a true friend of Jews and Hebrew Christians.

The Jews were often offended at the warmth and love with which we treated those who hated Jews; they were shocked, and often left our meetings when they heard us praying openly for the anti-Jewish authorities. They were angry because we maintained good relations with anti-Semitic clergymen and laymen.

Pope Gregory VII once said: "Just as a spiritual thing cannot be seen except through its earthly being, and just as the soul cannot function without a body, so religion cannot work without a Church. But if the Church has a body, then it also has its sins and weaknesses." Anti-Semitism is one of the many weaknesses suffered by the body of the Church; but it is not an isolated phenomenon. It has its diametric opposite: Jewish chauvinism and contempt for Christian people and for Christian Jews.

We must tolerate the weaknesses of the weak, and endeavour to cure them with love. In some cases we have succeeded in doing this. We believe that love can triumph over hatred.

Confucius wrote: "I have seen a man trying to put out a great fire with a cup of water. He failed, and concluded that water does not extinguish fire. The fool! A cup of water cannot extinguish a fire, but a great deal of water can."

The drop of love which we possess cannot extinguish evil in this world, but a great deal of love will do so. In any case, we do not believe that there is any sense in being angry with the stick from which you receive your blows. Be indignant with the man who wields the stick. Your enemy is driven by hatred; hatred must be hated, but not the man.

There are reasons why people turn against the Jews; one of these reasons is to be found in the sins of which Jews, like other nations, are guilty. There are undoubtedly many more reasons, which have their source in the evils of the anti-Semite's heart. We need understanding, and must try as far as possible to remove the causes, but we must not hate the anti-Semites.

In many cases I have seen that it is sufficient for a number of Jew-haters to encounter Jews who are devout Christians, for their anti-Semitism to disappear as though it had never existed.

How many of us are personally prepared to subscribe to the old saying that an enemy is a treasure that has fallen from heaven? We must care for him as a means to aid our own spiritual progress. Without anti-Semitism, the state of Israel would never have come into being; Theodore Herzl, the founder of Zionism, was aware of this. Without anti-Semitism, the Jewish Christians would never have had an opportunity of practising the valuable virtues of patience and love of one's enemies. Our enemies are our benefactors. They are in truth only their own enemies, because they are preparing their own hell.

As far as the slaughtered and tortured members of our people are concerned, we are every bit as distressed at losing them as other Jews are; but our sorrow is appeased by the hope of resurrection and the hope that in the Kingdom of God all injustices will be made good.

Christ's martyrs among the Jewish people

I have said something about Feinstein, who in his death testified to his faith. I believe that in the better world to which he went, he is still interested in me and in the work which he set on foot. How else am I to explain the remarkable coincidence that on two occasions before I was sentenced to protracted terms of imprisonment, I preached on the Sunday prior to my arrest in Jassy of all places, from the pulpit where he had preached; and I lived in the house which was still permeated by his spirit, and received strength from his example? I must now mention other Jews who in their love of Jesus set little store by their lives.

The first of these was Vladimir Davidmann. He was the son of a rabbi in Balti. It was intended that he should follow in his father's footsteps, and become a teacher in Israel.

Being indifferent, as are most Christian Jews, about the conflicts between the various Christian confessions—which arose at the time when the Jews were not yet incorporated in the Church, and which they consider they would be better advised not to participate in, unless they can bring about conciliation—he joined the Greek Orthodox Church, at that time the dominant one in Rumania. Such was the nature of his soul that he would have felt equally at home in the Lutheran Church, or among the Baptists, because he was attracted by the essence of Christianity, and not by its conditioned history. He regarded the principles separating the various confessions as a disguise to conceal pride, material and political interests, and personal ambitions, which are the real sources of schism.

From his earliest years he had been taught to read aloud the long and daily prayers of the Jews, in which the thirteen articles of faith of the Mosaic belief are pronounced. One of them runs: "I believe in perfect faith that all the words of the prophets are true." But he noticed that some of these words, which according to this pronouncement were supposed to be true, were concealed from him, for instance the fifty-third chapter of Isaiah. Vladimir's teacher ignored this passage, but Vladimir himself read it, realising that the prophecies concealed a mystery.

One day, out of curiosity, he entered the Greek Orthodox cathedral in the town. The magnificent service made a deep impression on him, and he repeated his visit. First of all he pondered these things, and later on he realised that there was a connection between the service he had witnessed in the church and the fact that the Jews suppressed some of the texts in the Scripture, and he was convinced that the promised Messiah had come. Jesus was that Messiah.

Not surprisingly, the rumour spread in the town that the young Jew with ringlets and a kaftan was often to be seen in the Greek Orthodox church. When he refused to obey his family's demand that he should put an end to this "aberration", his father kept him locked up in the house for six months. As soon as he was released, he sought contact with the priests, left home with nothing but the clothes he was wearing, and made his way to the monastery at Dobrovăt. Here he was baptised. On the day he was to be baptised, he was lying in bed suffering from pneumonia. Nevertheless, he went through with the ceremony, and emerged from the cold baptismal water completely restored.

His parents, who had made great efforts to locate him, discovered his hiding-place. They abducted him from the monastery, and brought him back home. Several orthodox rabbis were gathered in the house, and they decided to punish the "traitor" with death. But that very night thieves broke into the house of the Rabbi Davidmann. In the ensuing confusion, Vladimir managed to escape. He made his way to the monastery of Neamtul in Moldavia.

One day, as he was walking near the monastery, his young brother, a fanatic, who had tracked him down, attacked and wounded him.

When he had recovered, he made his way to Bucharest, so that his family should be unable to trace him. Here he was admitted to a school where he was to learn church music, subsequently continuing his studies in Cernauti.

In 1937 he was on his way to this town to take his final exam. In the train he was reading a book of prayers, while his travelling companions were discussing various worldly matters. They noticed that he was reading a prayer book, and occasionally making the sign of the Cross, and they began to mock him. Thereupon Vladimir knelt down, and started to read the prayer book from the first page, this time aloud. The mockers were silenced. When he had finished, they apologised for their behaviour, and asked him, as a sign that he had forgiven them, to read the whole prayer again.

The night after his arrival in Cernauti he had a dream, in which he saw a desolate landscape filled with repulsive animals. He was riding on the back of one of these animals. In the face of another monster he recognised an uncle, who bit him with all his might. Suddenly he saw a saint, dressed in shining ecclesiastical robes, descending a luminous ladder. He recognised him as St. Seraphim, whose ikon he had seen in the monastery. In his hand the saint held a chalice, on which were the words "Consuming Fire", inscribed in Yiddish. Flames poured out of the chalice, filling the air. Then the vision vanished, and Vladimir saw nothing but a beautiful green meadow. When he awoke, he wrote a letter to an acquaintance in Bucharest, in which he recounted what had happened on his journey, and described his dream.

The next day, Vladimir was shot and mortally wounded by his uncle who was inflamed by religious fanaticism. He lived for only a few hours. The matter was widely reported in the newspapers. But the system of "hush money" was firmly established in Rumania in those days: the authorities and the press were bribed, and no one was punished.

The death of Vladimir Davidmann was not without its fruits: as he lay dying he was nursed by his sister, a girl of about seventeen. She was converted when she saw her brother's steadfastness in the faith, while dying the death of a martyr. She, too, was baptised into the Greek Orthodox Church.

She figured in an unusual episode which deserves to be mentioned.

When the German-Rumanian troops occupied Cernauti in 1941, this girl, together with thousands of other Jews, was deported to Kamentz-Podolsk in the Ukraine. Suddenly, SS troops arrived on the scene and set about massacring the whole camp. But killing ten thousand people is no easy task: graves had to be dug, and the bodies of the murdered Jews had to be buried by those who were awaiting their turn to be killed. This took two or three days, and Maria Davidmann, with the others, was awaiting her turn. Unexpectedly, a German officer came up to her, and without any preamble asked her: "Are you a Christian?" Astonished, she answered that she was. The officer then told her: "You are not going to die. Follow me." At the risk of his own life, this officer took her back to Cernauti, thus saving her from an almost certain death.

It is probable that a German soldier, a Christian, who was on duty at the time, heard her talking about Jesus to the other Jews who were waiting to be slaughtered. As she was speaking in Yiddish—a language which is akin to German, and which Germans can understand—he would have realised that she was a disciple of Jesus. He must have reported this secretly to his commanding officer, whom he knew to be a Christian (I also have met a Gestapo officer who was a child of God), and this man made up his mind to save her, even at the risk of his own life.

From Cernauti Maria was taken to Bucharest—far from the theatre of war—where she was safe.

I have often talked to her. She was a simple Christian, not remarkable for any special gift of grace or virtue. Most clergymen would have regarded her as one of the weaker vessels. I have often wondered why God performed this miracle for her. Could it have been for the sake of her brother? The apostle Paul writes that in his day the Jews, who were not even weak Christians but the enemies of the gospel, were loved for the sake of their forefathers, who had lived two thousand years before their time – Abraham, Isaac and Jacob. Is it possible that today, too, there are those who are loved and predestined by God to fulfil a special purpose, for the sake of a relative or a close friend who was strong in the faith? In the gospel we read that Jesus healed a man sick of the palsy, not for his own sake, but for the sake of the faith of his friends, who had carried him on a bed and placed him before the Saviour. Should we not learn to believe and love greatly for those who cannot do so? Theirs would be a great blessing.

But Feinstein and Davidmann were not the only ones: the Christian Jews had several martyrs. In Chishinau there lived a group who were very active. Their leaders, the engineer Tarlev, Trachtmann and Schmil Ordienski, were deported to Siberia because of their faith when the Russians arrived in Bessarabia in 1940, and there they were killed. In the hope that it may serve as a lesson to others, I will mention that this group lived in a state of acute conflict with the Baptist Church in the same town, a conflict which was based on purely personal grounds. The passions aroused in the leaders acerbated the conflict to the extent that members of the two groups would cut one another in the street. But in Siberia, leaders of the Jewish Christian group died side by side with the pastor of the Baptist congregation in Chishinau, Bushilă, for their faith. Why do we have to wait for the enemy to make us see reason?

I remember young Friedmann, a Christian Jew from Jassy, who was killed in the pogrom. The Jews were herded into a cattle truck, which was bursting at the seams. Friedmann peeped out through a little window, and someone on the platform who happened to catch sight of him told us later that his face shone like an angel's. A German soldier fired at him, and mortally wounded him.

During the war, Jews were forbidden to travel. It was not until later that I was allowed to make my way to Jassy to reorganise the Christian Jewish community there, which after the pogrom consisted only of women. On this occasion I visited Friedmann's mother. I tried to comfort her, and to tell her of Jesus. It proved impossible. Her husband and all her four sons had been killed on one and the same day by people who called themselves Christians. Her heart was like a stone.

God, who inspired the author of Exodus to write: "And Moses spake so unto the children of Israel: but they hearkened not unto Moses for anguish of spirit, and for cruel bondage" (Exod. 6.9), and also inspired Job to exclaim: "Oh that my grief were thoroughly weighed, and my calamity laid in the balances together! For now it would be heavier than the sand of the sea" (Job. 6.2–3), would also find an excuse for this woman, whose heart had been completely hardened. She had but one answer to everything: "If God existed, then he would have restored at least one of my five dear ones to me."

I could not persist, but withdrew, in deference to this unspeakable sorrow.

Shall I tell the story of Marica? When the Kallai government ordered the deportation of Hungarian Jews to the death camps of Auschwitz, Treblinka and elsewhere, exceptions were made of Christian Jews who had been born to baptised parents. Marica, who had studied theology at the Reformed Faculty, was one of these. But she withheld the secret of her birth, which would have given her this privilege, and voluntarily reported at the assembly point from which the Jews were to be deported. She wished to accompany the others to the death camp, so that right to the end she could bear witness of her faith to the victims of anti-Semitic persecution, and then die with other members of her race. Marica was one of the few who survived Auschwitz. Together with other women survivors she made her way through Bucharest en route for Israel. They called her "Saint Marica". In Israel, the unavoidable psychological reaction after the strain of such a heroic deed followed. The Bible does not tell us what happened to the three young men after they left the fiery furnace. It is better so. But God is not unjust, and has not forgotten her sacrifice. A simple understanding of the laws of psychology would have saved her from much depression.

Christian peasants from Cetatea Alba, who were forced to stand by and watch, helpless and in tears, while SS troops executed Jews from this town, have described how a young Jewess, hitherto unknown to them, called out to other Jews as they faced the firing-squad: "We are expiating the sin of not receiving Jesus, the true Messiah of our race. But believe in Him and you will awake happy in His paradise."

There are many Christian Jews who suffered imprisonment for their faith. Pastor Milan Haimovici was imprisoned for many years under the Communist regime because of his faith, and those who were imprisoned with him, including anti-Semites, had only words of praise for him, calling him a hero. When he was released he was met with indifference, and even hatred, by his colleagues, for whose sake he had even suffered the torture of having his feet placed on glowing coals, but without informing against them. His martyrdom was disparaged even by those who preferred not to suffer for Jesus, but this only makes his suffering all the more glorious.

It would of course be impossible for me to mention everyone. Suzana Golder was arrested when she was only seventeen because she preached the Word of God to some Fascists, who promptly took her off to their headquarters. The commanding officer started his interrogation by giving her a violent blow across the face. She immediately turned her other cheek, and asked: "Won't you hit me again?"—"What sort of question is that?" the officer asked. She replied: "Jesus, whom you say you worship, commanded that when a man strikes you on one cheek, you shall turn the other." The man who had struck her was so astonished that he immediately ordered her to be set free.

This is not the only incident of this nature. Another Christian Jew, Bianca, was forced to undergo great suffering because she distributed the gospel to some Russian soldiers. It would be unjust not to remember Rumanian brothers and sisters, whose names cannot for obvious reasons be mentioned at the present time, who spent years in prison because they had faithfully helped the Christian Mission to the Jews. Countless young Christian Jews were ill-treated by their parents on account of their Christian faith.

Generally speaking, Christian Jews are forced to suffer a great deal. They suffer at the hands of some of their own people, who do not understand them. They are forced to suffer at the hands of the "Christian" anti-Semites, in whose eyes they are, and will always remain, "dirty Jews"; and they suffer at the hands of the atheists.

Hebrew Christians are often humiliated by their co-nationals, but this should not surprise us in view of the attitude that so-called Christians, with their disgusting anti-Semitism, have stirred up in the souls of the Jews. The most important anti-Semitic organisations in Rumania were named the Legion of the Archangel Michael (despite the fact that in the Bible the Archangel is referred to, in Daniel, Chapter 12, as the protector of the children of Jewish people) and the National Christian Defence League.

I asked one of the leaders of an organisation of this kind what he meant by the word Christian. His definition was: "Being a Christian means being against the dirty Jews." And this man was against the Jews not only in word but also in deeds, with his stick. It is not surprising, therefore, that at the opposite pole, the idea has arisen that being a Jew means being opposed to Christianity.

The human mind is perverted by noxious complexes of many kinds, and we Christian Jews, who stand at the cross-roads where many a violent storm rages, are compelled to suffer at the hands of many people.

But is this suffering not for our own good?

St. Gregory of Nazianzus wrote of the Christian Church in the fourth century, which was liberated by Constantine the Great: "We have lost the greatness and the strength we had during our persecution and troubles."

Jerome wrote in similar terms: "From the time of the coming of the Saviour until now, that is to say, from the time of the Apostles up to the present, the congregation of Christ, after being born and growing, became great during its persecutions and was crowned with martyrdom. But since the Christians have become strong, this congregation has in truth increased because of its tradition and wealth, but has decreased in virtue."

I am convinced that the humble position of the Christian Jews is ordained by God. Through many tribulations they are prepared, not only to enter into God's kingdom, but also to play a leading role in the work of establishing it. The Apostle Paul tells us that the receiving of the Jews, their conversion to Jesus, will be life from the dead (Rom. 11.15). If carrying a heavy cross today did not mean preparation for future glory, our good Lord would not allow us to endure so much suffering.

Might it not be true that many Christians in the western

world are no longer persecuted because they no longer frighten Satan, because they are unfaithful to Jesus? The Christian Jews should be grateful to God for persecution and for the martyrs they have fostered in so many parts of the world.

One Christian Jew, the well-known professor of theology, Neander, has written: "Oh, what soft-minded and weak witnesses, with what cold feelings, we are, who nevertheless still call ourselves Christians! We must feel ashamed when we remember the days of Ignatius and Polycarp [Christian martyrs of the second century who were devoured by lions] and others, and we shall wish that we had died a thousand times for Christ. Most of us, even the greatest theologians, are very different from the martyrs. We do not like to be looked at askance, we push aside any difficulty we may have with regard to the truth, and yet we are people of reputation and great theologians, but only in words—not in deed."

God grant that both the Christian Jews and the Gentile Christians will take these reproaches to heart, and openly condemn the crimes of this world, at the risk of having to suffer the martyr's death!

We are proud that among the Jews, too, the blood of martyrs has been shed for the sake of Jesus. Let us learn from these our noble pioneers to carry our cross, and to carry it with joy!

3

ARGUMENTS FOR THE RESURRECTION

Encounter on a Train

THE YEAR WAS 1939. I was travelling by train from Cernauti to Bucharest, and on the seat opposite sat a renowned rabbi from Cernauti. When he saw me reading the Bible, he asked me who I was.

"A Christian Jew," I told him.

He was highly astonished. "If you are a Jew, why did you become a Christian?"

"Because I believe that Jesus is the Saviour."

"But, young man, how can you maintain anything of the kind? What makes you believe that Jesus was our Messiah?"

"In this Bible there are many proofs, and I can't reel them all off at once for you in the train. But there is one proof above all others: His resurrection. If Jesus had been a deceiver, or a man who deluded himself, God would not have performed the miracle of raising Him from the dead."

"I can see that you are a grown man. However can you believe that nonsense, that Jesus rose from the dead?"

"Rabbi, the proofs of Jesus's resurrection are so convincing that if you promise to listen calmly to me for twenty minutes, then I promise you that you too will believe in His resurrection from the dead."

"I should like to see that happening, a young man convincing a rabbi that Jesus rose from the dead. Go ahead, young man, I'll give you twenty minutes."

Here are some of the main arguments I quoted to the rabbi.

"What is the source of our knowledge of ancient history? The historians of their age, among them men like Homer, Herodotus and Julius Caesar. What is the source of our knowledge of the doings of Jesus? Contemporary historians: their names are Matthew, Mark, Luke, John, Paul and so on. Why should we believe some historians and not others?

"Our intelligence should behave like an impartial court of law, carefully and competently weighing the statements of witnesses. In evaluating evidence we must consider not only what the witness says, but also his character and his trustworthiness. The credibility of the historians who described the life of Jesus is undoubtedly much greater than that of other historians. For who were the latter? Generally, they were paid to write by a royal personage, and their aim was not to make known the truth. They desired to flatter their master, their people, or the social class to which they belonged. By contrast, the historians who wrote the Gospels are of an entirely different stature. They risked loss of liberty and death for what they wrote. Matthew died as a martyr in Abyssinia, John was condemned to slave labour on the island of Patmos, and Paul was beheaded in Rome. Peter was crucified head downwards. No impartial court would lightly dismiss the evidence of witnesses ready to suffer such hardships for what they assert. All of them declare unanimously that they were convinced by seeing, hearing and touching, of the reality of Jesus's resurrection from the dead."

The rabbi attempted to interrupt. I reminded him that he had promised to let me have my say.

"I know that this argument can be contradicted. What the other historians relate are things that can easily be understood and believed. They write about wars, court intrigues, kings' favourites, plots, murder, things that happen even today, whereas the writers of the Gospels tell us of things that run counter to our human experience. Among other things, they write about a virgin birth, of the healing of lepers by a simple touch, of walking on the water, of the feeding of a great multitude with a few loaves, of men rising from the dead, and finally of Jesus's own resurrection, which was followed by His ascension into heaven. All these things come into the category of miracles, whereas we are modern people who no longer believe in miracles."

Tradition tells us that Jesus spoke from the time of His birth. This has been regarded by rationalists as pure fantasy. Had this conversation taken place thirty years later, I could have told the rabbi that in the 1960s, papers all over the world reported that a child had been born in Yugoslavia which spoke and answered questions from the day it was born. The evangelists were cautious men, and anxious not to make the gospel difficult to understand, and they did not record whether Jesus spoke from His birth. How people would have mocked the Gospels if they had written this! But today an event that is so unusual in the natural order of things has taken place before our very eyes.

In 1963 the newspapers reported that a French boy of about sixteen, when his abdomen was opened up, was found to be "pregnant". What should have been his twin had developed inside his body. How the rationalists would have laughed if the evangelists had written that a man had been pregnant!

"As to the miracles that Jesus performed," I told the rabbi, "they occurred in the sphere of the exceptional, whose existence cannot be denied. In everyday life it is not only ordinary things that occur. A man who does not believe in miracles is not a realist.

"Furthermore, men consider as miracles things which a person with greater than average intelligence or muscular power can do, and which a weak person with an ordinary intelligence is incapable of doing. Missionaries who have worked among primitive tribes record that the savages regard them as miracle-workers; and this is not surprising, since primitive people spend hours rubbing two pieces of wood together in order to produce a spark, whereas the missionary knows how to produce fire from a box of matches. He can even make stinking water burn. How is the savage to know that this stinking water is petrol? The writer Pearl Buck tells us that when she told peasant women in backward parts of China that in England there were houses built on top of one another, and that carriages moved through the streets without being drawn by horses, one of the women whispered: 'What a lie! That sort of thing is impossible.' With sixty Spaniards under his command, Cortez conquered the powerful Aztec kingdom, because he appeared to the people he conquered to be a miracle-maker. In the first place, the very appearance of the Spaniards was miraculous. Never before had the Aztecs seen white men. Secondly, the newcomers possessed miraculous things which the Aztecs had never seen before, horses and firearms. And so a huge kingdom fell into the hands of a few adventurers without a struggle.

"Jesus had a spiritual force such as no other person has ever possessed. It is not surprising that He was capable of performing miracles. Being exceptional, He could do unique things, which would have been impossible for ordinary men.

"It is foolish to be prejudiced, and declare that miracles are impossible, and to reject them without carefully examining the evidence of people as trustworthy as the apostles. Rabbi, you cannot avoid miracles. Either you can believe in Jesus's miraculous resurrection from the dead, or you have to believe in another miracle which is still greater—namely, that an effect exists without a cause, because if Jesus did not rise from the dead, the existence of the universal Church would be such a miraculous happening.

"Let us see how things stand: Jesus wrote no book, nor, while He lived on earth, did He establish anything but a very insignificant sect within Judaism, a sect consisting of a few people who were unlearned, and who were not considered reputable citizens—sinful men, publicans and fallen women. Finally, one of his closest followers betrayed Him, another denied Him, and the others deserted Him. He died on a cross, abandoned, and apparently despairing, because as He hung on the cross He cried out: 'My God, my God, why hast thou forsaken me?' After His death He was buried, a large stone was placed in front of His sepulchre, and guards were posted. Meanwhile, His former disciples remained in hiding, behind locked doors, and their only concern was to escape a death similar to that of their Master. This was how Jesus's life on earth ended. If Jesus did not rise, how has the Christian Church come into being?

"We have an explanation. On the third day, Jesus came back to life from the dead, and appeared on numerous occasions to His apostles, assuring them that it was really Himself they saw. They came together again; the risen Jesus worked with them guiding them and giving them power to do signs and wonders. The very same cowardly Peter who had previously denied any knowledge of Jesus with curses and oaths, stood up in the marketplace in Jerusalem, courageously testifying that he had seen the risen Jesus. The other apostles did so, too. Risking death, they travelled from one country to another, sealing with a martyr's death their conviction that Jesus had risen. In this way, the universal Church was born, it has grown, and it has survived, despite persecution and the unworthiness of its members. If you are not prepared to admit that Jesus has risen from the dead, then this tremendous effect, which the Christian Church represents—a Church that has survived for two thousand years, and has millions of members—is an effect without a cause. It takes a greater naïvety to accept the existence of such an effect without cause than to admit that Christ has really risen.

"When a man enters a tall building, it might be a good idea, before climbing the stairs to the tenth floor, to go down first into the cellar and make sure that the foundations are sound. But why should it be necessary to do this? The fact that the building is standing is proof of the strength of the foundations. The foundation stone on which the Christian Church was built is the resurrection of Jesus. The large, well-known building founded on this stone has stood for two thousand years, and has resisted tremendous earthquakes. After all, in every sphere of life, it is common practice to draw conclusions from effect to cause. The existence of the Church is a proof that Christ has risen.

"Let us proceed to another argument with regard to the

resurrection of Jesus. Nowhere do we find that the enemies of the primitive Church at any time denied that the sepulchre of Jesus was found to be empty on Easter morning. It would have been quite natural for an investigation to have been set on foot, to discover whether the body had been stolen or desecrated. The reaction of the Jewish priests does not contradict the assertion that the grave was empty; they merely told the soldiers who had guarded the sepulchre to spread the rumour that His disciples had come during the night, while they were asleep, and stolen the body. Now, if they were asleep, then how could they have identified the thieves? Augustine rightly asks: 'Does the synagogue introduce us to witnesses who were asleep when this deed was carried out?' If the Jewish priests really believed that Jesus's disciples had stolen the body, why were they not arrested, interrogated, and punished?

"A strong movement must be carried forward by a strong impetus. The strong movement that has lasted for two thousand years, and which has had a world-wide effect, based on the belief in the resurrection of Jesus, cannot have been the product of hallucination, as none of Jesus's disciples were men who suffered from hallucinations, certainly not Doubting Thomas and the practical businessman Matthew, nor such men of the sea as Andrew, nor the cautious Nathaniel, nor Peter with his weak character. Only an event as tremendous as a real resurrection could have produced an impetus capable of starting a movement of this kind. Nor must we forget that during the first thirty years after this event, most of Jesus's disciples suffered a violent death, and many of them were condemned to death precisely because they maintained that Jesus had risen from the dead. These things cannot have been invented.

"Under the very noses of the Jewish priests, Jesus's apostles start to preach to the Jewish people, and in this way they come into conflict with the authorities, as they declare that Jesus is the Messiah, a fact which was proved by His resurrection. Any sensible person may ask: 'Would it be possible to launch a movement of this kind, and recruit thousands of supporters in a single day, if the dead body of Jesus had really existed?' Peter preached his first sermon only a few hundred yards from Jesus's sepulchre. If Jesus's enemies had been in a position to prove that His body was still there, the sermon would have been a failure, and would never have persuaded thousands of people to be baptised. But their enemies were powerless: Jesus was not in the tomb.

"The apostles did not visit the tomb of Jesus, because it had no significance as far as they were concerned, and because they would not be interested in it. (Saul of Tarsus, after he was converted, came to Jerusalem and met the apostles, but was not concerned with visiting the tomb, not even out of mere respect.) Nor did His enemies investigate the tomb, to convince themselves and convince others that Jesus was still there. This is yet another proof that Jesus really rose from the dead. A great many people undertake pilgrimages to the tombs of minor saints. Even though the first apostles knew of this custom in Israel (Matt. 23.29), they were not interested in visiting Jesus's tomb, because they knew that it was empty.

"All this was so universally accepted that the disciples started preaching, not in a provincial town, where it would be difficult to check their statements, but in Jerusalem itself, arousing the enthusiasm of thousands of people and—what was still more remarkable—facing enemies who were powerless, because they were not in a position to deny that Jesus's tomb was empty. When the priests maintained that the body of Jesus had been stolen by the apostles, anyone could have answered them: 'Why don't you arrest and sentence the men who have carried out this theft?'

"The suggestion that Jesus did not die on the cross, but merely fell into a deep swoon, and recovered consciousness in the cool tomb, is still more ridiculous. How could He have pushed aside the stone, and overpowered the guards, after so much suffering? Could He have gone anywhere, naked as He was? He could have sought shelter only with one or other of His disciples. Had He done this, however, His disciples would have realised that He had not risen from the dead.

Would they have really given their lives for a lie which they themselves had hatched?

"We are compelled to believe what the Gospel writers say, because they reveal such naïvety when relating terrible things about themselves. What induced the apostles to spread abroad by word of mouth and in their writings that their leader, Peter, was a man whom Jesus had called Satan, and that he had denied Him on the night that He was betrayed? The only motive I can discover is that they showed an uncompromising regard for the truth. The band of apostles is a collection of men who are guided by the truth. We can trust their evidence.

"The remarkable thing is that when the apostles affirm the resurrection of Jesus to an audience of doubters (even in those days people were sceptical about stories of angels, resurrections and so on, as we can see in Matthew, Chapter 22, verse 23, and Acts, Chapter 17, verse 32), they merely affirm, without producing a single confirmatory piece of evidence. This was possible because what they maintained was a well-known and undisputed fact among the inhabitants of Jerusalem. The risen Jesus, after all, had at one time appeared to five hundred persons, and these must have had about twenty thousand relatives and friends whom they told about it.

"The resurrection of Jesus can also be proved by two very famous conversions which could not be explained in any other way.

"The first was the conversion of James, the brother of Jesus, to a faith in Him as the Messiah. While Jesus lived on earth, James did not believe in Him, but considered Him to be mad. Josephus Flavius describes James as a very upright man. How was it possible that he became an apostle and martyr after the death of Jesus? Anyone reading James's letter (the Straw Epistle, as Luther calls it) will note that this is a Jewish letter, without any Christian characteristics. This leads us to realise that it was not the teaching of Jesus that made an impression on James, and brought about his conversion. What was the cause? It can only have been what we are told in the New Testament, that Jesus after His resurrection appeared to His brother, and that the latter admitted his mistake, and in remorse wrote the chapter in which he condemns his own former sin of judging and speaking about his brother.

"The second conversion was that of the rabbi Saul of Tarsus. This man had a vision on the road to Damascus, in which Jesus appeared to him and spoke to him, whereupon Saul immediately became a disciple. Would this have been possible on purely psychological grounds? Even though Mohammed were to appear to me ten times, I should tell myself that I was suffering from hallucinations, and I certainly should not become a Mohammedan. Why should things have turned out so differently for the man who was to become the future apostle Paul? He knew that Jesus's tomb was empty, without being able to find a plausible explanation for this fact, unless he admitted to himself that Jesus had risen. This was the crux of the matter: when he saw Jesus, the last shred of doubt disappeared. He was converted. He later made his way to Jerusalem, but he had not the slightest intention of going to the tomb in order to shed tears of remorse there. He knew it was empty. He discussed with the apostles how to preach the resurrection. It would have been a psychological impossibility for the apostles, being the sort of men they were, to discuss how best to preach a lie.

"And here is another argument: millions of sinners in the history of mankind have changed their mind and become holy people. This miracle is happening daily in the Church. If you ask these people how this miracle of rebirth happened, their answer is always that Jesus did it. It is certain that it is a living Jesus, not a dead one, who has brought about these new births. I am one of these people.

"The cumulative force of these arguments compels me to believe in the resurrection of Jesus. But let me turn to an argument from a person of real authority. Professor Theodor Mommsen, the great historian of the Roman Empire, wrote: 'The resurrection of Jesus is the event in ancient history which has been more conclusively proved than any other event.' That is all I need to tell you.

"There is something more. If a woman's husband is missing in a war and believed to be dead, and then one, two, three, four people, in fact countless people, come and tell her that they have seen him in a prisoner-of-war camp, then the wife will trust those people. We are in the same situation. Those who believed that Christ was dead, heard the witness of the women, of the apostles, of the disciples on the road to Emmaus, of five hundred people who had seen Him on the same day. After this it was only normal for them to believe that Jesus was no longer dead, but alive."

After I had finished speaking, the rabbi was silent for several minutes. Then he got up, opened the door, and said to me: "Even if He has risen, what has that to do with me?" And he walked out. When he returned to the compartment, neither he nor I spoke a word till we reached Bucharest.

During the tragic events of the war, this rabbi was killed by the Fascists.

Many years passed. One evening, during a week of evangelistic mission, the church was full to bursting. Instead of preaching a sermon, I told my listeners of my conversation with the rabbi. When I had finished, a young Jewish woman student came up to me and said: "You have convinced me, too, that Jesus is risen, but for me it means a great deal."

The same arguments affected two persons quite differently.

Returning for a moment to the rabbi, I must add that, generally speaking, I have found many rabbis very ill-prepared to answer our arguments. I once talked to one of the Berlin rabbis, who had fled to Rumania. I showed him the text in the ninth chapter of Isaiah, which foretells the coming into the world of the Messiah, declaring: "For unto us a child is born, unto us a son is given: and the government shall be upon his shoulder: and his name shall be called Wonderful, Counsellor, The mighty God, The everlasting Father, The Prince of Peace. Of the increase of his government and peace there shall be no end . . ." (Isa. 9.6–7). This passage contains an orthographical curiosity. In Hebrew, the letter M is written at the beginning and in the middle of a word with the sign מ, and only at the end of a word as a closed square. This orthography is rigidly adhered to throughout the Old Testament, except in one particular case. In this verse, in the word *lemarbe* (increase), a final M, ם, appears in the middle of the word. This orthographical mistake has never been corrected. A final M, ם, which should occur only at the end of the word is written in the middle of one.

I asked the rabbi if he could explain this, but he could give me no answer. I then told him of the Kabalistic tradition, that Isaiah put a ם in the middle of the word, in order to show the reader who was destined to understand it that the Divine Child of whom this prophecy speaks would be born of the closed womb of a virgin.

Many other arguments, which I personally consider more conclusive, would have made a far smaller impression on the rabbi than this one. He had no further counter-argument when I told him that the Messiah is the man who was born of the Virgin Mary, and when I explained that because the Messiah bears our sins, which according to the prophet Isaiah results in His being bruised, every person who recognizes that the Messiah is killed for our sins will no more bear his own guilt.

Among other rabbis I have even come across sympathy for Jesus. When I told an old rabbi that Jesus is the Messiah whose coming Isaiah had prophesied, he shook his head and said: "No! Jesus does not need to be accredited by Isaiah. Compared to Him, Isaiah is small. It is not because of Isaiah that the world believes in Jesus, but the other way round; because of Jesus, millions of people also appreciate Isaiah. Jesus is the sun."

Then there are other rabbis, who are rabbis merely by profession, as are many Christian priests and pastors.

I once spoke to a rabbi who was a liberal, and tried to convince him that Jesus was the Son of God. After listening politely, he answered: "You wish me to believe in the Son, but I don't even believe in the Father. If God existed, He would not have allowed my family to be killed in Auschwitz."

We discover modern theology

The moment came for our first encounter with English books of modern theology. We had not even known that modernists existed: the Bible was dear to us because it contained the message of Jesus. We accepted it, and regarded it as the word of God. We did not dissect it, or criticise it, but rather we allowed it to criticise us.

Now we heard and read about various human sources of the Bible which even contradicted one another, and that the Bible contained some things that were later additions. It was denied that Jesus had done wonderful things, or else His miracles were interpreted in such a way that in the end there was nothing left.

I was profoundly shocked. I know of a former preacher who, after reading a book by a Christian modernist, completely lost his faith, and even went so far as to write an anti-Christian, atheistic book himself. This man was separated from God for years. Other people, including myself after I had been released from prison, were able subsequently to help him to recover his faith.

Marx began as a Christian. Two liberal theologians, Bruno Bauer and Strauss, destroyed his faith.

Rumanian Christians are fundamentalists. I do not know a single modernist, nor do I know what benefits we could derive from modernism.

It is true that the Bible exhorts us to "sing unto the Lord a new song" (Ps. 96.1). Every century must compose its own song of praise to God in its own particular style. It is written in Leviticus, Chapter 9, verse 3, that the animal which is brought to the temple for sacrifice must be a *benshana*, "of the first year". I do not live in the first century nor in the Middle Ages, and it would not be normal for me to have religious ideas belonging to those times. There must be progress in our thinking about God, too.

So modernism is not modern: it is very ancient. The Syrian Codex Sinaiticus, a New Testament manuscript from the second century, refers to Jesus simply as "the son of

Joseph", and omits the story of the virgin birth, about which the man who wrote it probably knew nothing. Augustine considered it blasphemous to believe in the first three chapters of the Bible as the literal truth. Origen stated that the story of the Creation, as it stands, is absurd and contradictory. Luther said that he did not believe that God created man "*in einem Hui*", all at once.

There are, of course, passages in the Bible which are very primitive. Who would condone the methods used to diagnose and cure leprosy as described in Leviticus Chapter 13? Even the fundamentalists permit themselves their own modernism.

The fault of the real modernists is that they go too far: all of a sudden the liberties they take can no longer be distinguished from others merely quantitatively; they are different in quality.

Modernists deny miracles. In the twentieth century, when the word "impossible" no longer exists, they declare that miracles are impossible! The virgin birth, the miraculous healings, the feeding of the five thousand, the physical resurrection from the dead; are these so impossible? In nature, it is not only the usual that exists: Mozart, after all, was composing music at the age of four.

Christ belongs to the sphere where the unusual is natural.

The American biologist Löbhas fertilised sea urchins, and produced live specimens by chemical means, without the use of male semen. Would it not be possible for God to create out of man what the biologist can create out of a lower form of life?

At the beginning of this century there lived in the Ukraine a rabbi by the name of Hofetz Haim. When the first world war broke out, one of his disciples was arrested as a result of anti-Semitism, on the false charge that he was spying for Germany. The rabbi was summoned as a defence witness. He was ordered to take the oath, but he refused, saying: "I can never remember having told a lie in my life, but I refuse to take the oath, as I do not want to bring God's holy name into a testimony, as an untruth might slip in against my will."

The prosecutor was delighted to be rid of an awkward witness. But the defence needed him badly, and so the lawyer, a Russian, asked that the rabbi should be listened to as a source of information, and he declared: "Your honour, allow me to relate one episode from the life of this rabbi, so that you may understand that he is an outstanding man who can be believed, even without taking the oath."

The president gave his assent, and the lawyer continued: "One day the rabbi went from one Jewish shop to another, collecting gifts for poor Jews. A thief lay in wait for him. That evening, when his collecting-box was full, the thief approached the rabbi and said to him: 'Perhaps you could change ten roubles?' The rabbi, who was glad to be rid of so much small change, opened his box, but with a swift movement the thief seized it, and ran off with it.

"The rabbi was horrified, not because he had lost the money—he immediately made up his mind to make good the loss from his own pocket—but because of the serious sin the thief had committed by stealing the money that belonged to the poor. He ran after the thief as fast as his old legs could carry him, and cried out: 'You have not stolen this money, it is yours. I have given it to you as a gift. I have got the poor people's money at home.'"

In amazement the president of the court interrupted the lawyer and asked him: "Do you really believe this story?" The lawyer answered: "No, I don't." The judge interrupted him angrily: "Why do you tell us stories that you do not believe yourself? You are quite out of order."

The lawyer answered: "Your honour, please do not be angry. Has a story of this kind ever been told about yourself, about the prosecuting counsel, or about me? Several stories are told about us, but these are in tune with our characters and our habits. It may be said of me that I have chased a lot of women, that I have often been drunk, and that I have cheated at cards, more than I have really done. What a just and holy man this rabbi must be, for such legends to circulate about him!"

The significance of this story is clear enough: no medical

commission has ever established Mary's virginity; there is no written evidence, submitted by scientists, to support the miracles performed by Jesus. But this does not mean that we can reject the stories in the Gospels.

One day, when my son was so small that he could not possibly know anything about sex, or what a virgin is, he asked me: "Daddy, how was Jesus born?" I answered: "But I've told you many times—he was born in a stable, and laid in a manger." "That's not what I want to know," the child answered. "You always say: like father, like son. If Jesus was born just like us, then He would have been bad, like us. So He must have been born in quite a different way."

The men and women who knew Jesus had precisely the same feeling as my son. Those who believed in Him were convinced of His virgin birth.

If He was so good and innocent and pure, if He was such a unique person, why, then, should He not also have been born in a unique manner? Why should he not also have risen from the dead?

One day a distinguished personality in the Lutheran Church came to see me on an administrative matter. After we had settled the financial problems, I asked him if he believed in Jesus. He was horrified that I should have asked him, one of the country's leading laymen in the Church, a question of this kind. I asked him to overlook his annoyance, and answer my question. Finally he said: "There is no valid juridicial proof of Jesus's resurrection." I submitted the same evidence to him which I had submitted to the rabbi from Cernauti. I asked him to assume the role of judge, and to evaluate the juridicial quality of the arguments I had submitted. He confessed that he now believed in the resurrection, was converted and also brought his wife into the faith. Later he reproved the bishop for having nominated him to such a high church office before making sure that he was a true child of God.

If you, too, analyse the evidence, you will realise the truthfulness of what the Gospels tell. The Bible in itself contains proof that it is telling the truth. Modernism sins by reducing

Jesus to a human personality who was nothing more than a great leader, a martyr to the truth, but about whom we know really very little, since the Gospels are not to be trusted. Modernism is negative: it takes away people's faith, and gives them nothing in return.

Of course, criticism of biblical texts is necessary, but not in the sense understood by the liberal school of theology.

It is assumed that the Old Testament text has been violated by rabbis.

For instance the martyr Justin, the Christian philosopher from the second century, maintained that the original of Psalm 96, verse 10, is: "The Lord has become King on the tree", but that the text was subsequently modified by the Jews. And after Ezra, Chapter 6, verse 22, there should have been a passage which ran as follows: "And Ezra said unto the people: this Passover is your Saviour and your refuge. And if you believe, then it shall come into your hearts, that they shall humiliate Him in spite of the signs that He has done, and that afterwards we shall hope in Him again, and this place shall never be laid desolate, saith the Lord God of Hosts. But if you do not believe, and do not hear these words that are spoke of Him, you shall be despised of the heathen." It is hard to believe that Justin should have invented this passage.

The Talmud also relates that the seventy rabbis who produced the Greek translation called the Septuagint, although they all worked in separate places, were inspired by the Holy Spirit to alter certain passages, all in the same way, in order not to offend other nations and races. In this legend, as in all others, there is undoubtedly a grain of truth: the texts of the Old Testament have undergone various modifications with a view to concealing certain facts. Strangely enough, the Septuagint still exerts a strong influence on practically all the translators of the Bible, who are thus translating the texts wrongly, as the rabbis had intended in days gone by.

Anyone comparing the manuscripts of the New Testament from the various centuries will note that here, too, there has been a gradual tendency to discard more and more of the various revolutionary and social characteristics of the primitive Church.

But we possess the most important texts dealing with the life, miracles, suffering and resurrection of the Saviour, the texts dealing with the way to salvation. The efforts of some people to undermine the faith of millions are merely to be deplored.

But the honesty of the modernists is useful, even if their teachings are not well received; they stimulate others to seek the truth elsewhere.

We sought it in Christian mysticism.

The Bible is in part only a handful of notes of discussions which God entered into with Abraham, Moses, the prophets and Jesus, and of conversations which Jesus had with the apostles, when He lived on earth and after His glorification, and of the thoughts with which the Holy Spirit inspired them.

But has God become dumb? Is it not possible for us to hear His voice today also? Perhaps we, too, can become pure in heart, so that we can see Him?

I had already read a great many other theological books, but now I also read the modernistic ones, and I got the impression that their ideas were superficial. There is a great deal of vanity in these, as in any other profane books. Theologians quote one another, instead of purging their spirits of all that is unessential in this qualified history which has accumulated in the course of centuries, and going back to the original source of power.

In the second place, I got the impression that this Christian theology at best stops at Jesus. But Jesus Himself said: "No man cometh unto the Father, but by me" (John 14.6). He declares that it is not He Himself, but the Father, who is the goal. If we have come to the Father, whom the Mosaic Jews also seek, we should be able to give them a helping hand. We should be able to prove to them that Jesus is the way they must follow to reach their desired goal. If we get no further than Jesus, whom they contest, then our witness is of little interest to them.

Up till now, the Scriptures had been windows through which we could see the reality of God; now we had opened the windows, so that we could look on the God of reality.

Some of us called the new experience the Baptism of the Holy Spirit; others called it the second blessing, or any other name. Suddenly our eyes were opened, and we saw the nature of things, instead of knowing merely by logic and intelligent conception. We now saw many of the things which normally are invisible. This meant that like butterflies or angels we fluttered from one flower to another. "The wind bloweth where it listeth, and thou hearest the sound thereof, but canst not tell whence it cometh, and whither it goeth" (John 3.8). For this reason we were often misunderstood.

As it is with God, our thoughts became reality. In Hebrew *davar* means both "word" and "thing". The words of the Bible became more and more a reality in which we lived.

We broke away from the cycle of sin—forgiveness—fresh sin, in which many believers pass their whole lives. Like Paul, we forgot what lay behind us. Paul never forgot that he had been a persecutor of the Church, and he regretted it. But the power of the past to influence his present life became less and less. And in the measure in which he became a new creature, the old sins seemed less to have belonged to him, but to somebody else, to the old Saul of Tarsus who was dead. In the same way, we "forgot" the past, with its ugly sin. We lived a present with God.

When Jesus washed His disciples' feet, He also wiped them with a towel, because wet feet always indicate that they were once dirty and needed to be washed. But once they have been dried, feet are clean. The Bible tells us that in Canaan Jesus turned water into the best wine; but old wine is the best. Jesus transformed water not into new wine, but into wine that was already old, that had been in existence for a long time. We were not justified by being converted, but in our conversion our eyes were opened, so that we could see a purity which we had already possessed long ago: we saw that we had always been pure in His eyes.

Our ideas took a new turn: we realised that we now partook

of eternal life, not by believing in Jesus, but that we had always had a special form of life, eternal life, because we were destined from eternity to be God's children. It is impossible to distinguish, at an early stage, the embryo of an ape from that of a man. At a certain moment the difference becomes visible, but it has always been there. Mary Magdalene, during her life of sin, was indistinguishable from any other courtesan, but she had always been one of God's elect. Her conversion was the moment when the difference was seen. We suddenly recognised, when the veil was taken from our eyes, our elder brother, Jesus, whom we had known long ago. "To know is to recognise," said Plato. We had proof of this.

We all live without remembering anything of our very early childhood, of our dreams or even of seventy-five per cent of what we do when we are awake. Why then should we nurture only the remembrance of our past sins?

Just as Jesus never made any mention of His early life before He was thirty years old, so we, too, did not stop at what had been, but every day we entered rejoicing into the holy of holies.

In me this release was caused by a very simple event, which I now recount for the first time. I was sitting writing in my study. In the room was all I held dear on earth: my wife, my children, my books. Suddenly the light went out; there had been a fuse. I could see nothing, and a great fear came over me. "One day," it flashed through my mind, "everything will be dark, I shall die, and my eyes will be closed. I shall be lost to all I now love." It is difficult to explain rationally the feeling of fear that flooded over me for a split second. But at once I realised the great store of riches I could enjoy in the darkness as well as in the light—the consciousness of I, the blessing of thought. Feverishly I examined myself. God, Christ, the angels, hope of eternal life, faith, all remained, even in the dark. They would be with me, too, at the moment when my eyes closed in death.

Like lightning, the thought struck me that things in this life are like the fabric of a dream: they are very easily dissolved.

It was then that I realised that the true nature of things is this quality of not being.

King Lisimachus surrendered when he was surrounded by the Scythians, forced to do so by hunger and thirst. After eating, he exclaimed: "How brief was the pleasure for which I sacrificed life and freedom!" So, in that fraction of a second, I realised that the soul tends to be attracted by the body, and neglects its great partner, God, who loves us with eternal love.

At that moment I passed over to the state where I lived the truth about the relative value of things, instead of merely knowing it. What I love in my human existence is transient, and one day it will have to be left behind. But the Divine Being, in which I have received a part through Jesus, is eternal. I experienced the reality of this myself, and for me the light would never be extinguished.

The words of the Scriptures: "Ye are gods" (Ps. 82.6), became a reality to me.

Light also represents a certain mass: when light falls on a plate, it brings a certain amount of power to bear on it. Sunbeams bring with them the mass of the sun: light is not an insubstantial messenger of the sun, but a part of the sun itself which comes to us. In many ways, likewise, we are not merely heralds of God's light, but God Himself; in a humble form we are divine sparks scattered about the world to bring light.

This conviction of the majesty of God's child has never since left me. I thought, as did the first Christians, from whom we have received the expression: "He who sees a brother, sees God."

When I thought of Jesus, I no longer thought of Him from the verses of the Bible. I entered into a reality where His majesty was visible. As long as there are Jews, Jesus will be their king, whether they recognise Him or not.

This experience had a different starting-point in the case of other brothers and sisters; but many were raised by the Spirit to new faith.

A Catholic priest, who was present at one of our meetings, said: "I have spent an evening among the first Christians."

The talks we had together in our gatherings took a new turn. We no longer talked about God, but from God.

Jesus now appeared to me in a new light. The sacrifices in the Jewish temple were consumed with fire. The sacrifice of Jesus, too, was consumed with the fire of love, which made us one with Him. Fire transforms all things into flames. In this way His sacrifice ceased to be a sacrifice made by one person for another. We are in Christ Jesus. As His elect, we were in Him also when He hung on the Cross.

When we looked at His Cross, we no longer thought of the use our souls could make of His suffering, for then we should have been like the soldiers who divided His garments among them. With such a good Saviour, salvation follows of itself. We asked ourselves another question: What are the reasons for which He allowed Himself to be crucified, so that we also may sacrifice ourselves for them and "fill up that which is behind of the afflictions of Christ in my flesh" (Col. 1.24)? In other words, how can we recruit for His service a host of loving followers, who are prepared to suffer?

From now on a fire burned within us, as it did in the disciples on the road to Emmaus. "Snowflakes cannot fall on a hot stove", says an Indian proverb. The coldness of this world could no longer harm us, although we had to pass through bitter times.

We tried not to let love be frittered away in sentimentality, endeavouring rather to manifest it in what St. Francis de Sales so beautifully described as "the ecstasy of acts".

Religious meditation now received still greater emphasis. We knew that the time spent in meditation was not wasted. It is, after all, better to think for a whole day than to work in vain for a whole week.

In the supreme moment of bliss the object of meditation, the meditation itself, and the person meditating, became one in such a way that meditation no longer became a conscious act. God was working in the unfathomable depths of the soul, which never reach to the surface of our consciousness.

Those who have had an experience of this kind are often asked: "But do you no longer sin?"

In our congregation great sins were still committed; I, too, committed great sins, even after I had had various mystical experiences. I shall not explain this, as I am much too small a person, but instead I shall let Meister Eckhardt speak: "Sin which is committed is not sin if we repent of it . . . He who has truly subjected himself to the will of God need not even wish not to have encountered the sin into which he fell. Not of course to the extent to which the sin is directed against God, but because through it you are in bondage to a still greater love, and you are cast down and humiliated . . . But if a man arise and entirely abandon his sins, faithful God will ensure that that man will be as though he had never fallen into sin, and He will not for a moment punish him for his sins. Even though his sins should be so numerous as those the whole of mankind might have committed, God will never punish him, and his relationship with God will be as intimate as God has ever entered into with any man. If man is prepared to do that now, God will not consider what has been. God is the God of the present. He is prepared to accept you as you are today. In this way He receives you not as the person you have been, but as the person you are now."

There is no danger in this doctrine, provided we do not draw Luther's conclusion from it, "*Peccator fortiter*"—Sin greatly!

The Holy Spirit of God, on the other hand, reminded me that at a time when I had been a high official in a certain company, I had often acted incorrectly. But the Devil prevented me from making a clean breast of things. When I went to see my former boss, in order to confess, I found him in a despondent mood. He greeted me with the words: "You were the only honest employee I had. Today I have been told that one of my confidential clerks has stolen a large sum of money from me." This man had suffered a great blow, and this was obviously not the right moment to speak to him about my own former dishonesty. But I was anxious not to have it weighing on my conscience. After a few days I wrote a confession, and offered to return what I had appropriated dishonestly, bit by bit.

Not only did he refuse to accept the money, but he told the big-time Jewish millionaires with whom he was on friendly terms, of my conversion. He became a Christian, together with his wife and son. Throughout the whole war I was able to devote my energies to preaching the gospel, because he, as well as a number of others, had arranged for me to receive a small monthly allowance.

4

THE FASCIST PERIOD

The beginning of the persecution

WHEN OLD PASTOR Adeney left us, he was replaced by a young man, Pastor Stevens. Both he and his wife were Christians who led very pure lives, and wished to spread the light around them. Their way of life testified to that correct Christianity which was common in England, but unknown in our part of the world, where even people who had been converted permitted themselves to do things which in the West would have been considered unworthy of a Christian. Their fairness and sincerity gave us much food for thought. We keep thankfulness to them. They left for what was meant to be a short vacation. But they could not return any more. Rumania had been taken over by a gang of anti-Semitic fanatics, whose hands were stained with a great deal of Jewish blood. They called themselves the Legionaires.

At that time the head of the Anglican Jewish Mission was a young priest called Roger Allison, a man we all remembered for his great humility. The humble man is strong in the Lord: by reducing himself to nothing, the humble man, joined with God, makes not two beings but one.

During the time he was our shepherd, our little community increased greatly. But we were also in great danger. If we went into the town, we never knew whether we should come back. The Legionaires were hunting the Jews in the streets, and arresting them on all sorts of trumped-up charges. On many occasions I was only a hand's breadth from death.

I should like to relate two episodes.

One Sunday afternoon I was sitting in my flat. A meeting

of young people was taking place in the church. Suddenly a breathless young man burst into my room, shouting: "Come down to the church at once! There is a terrible disturbance going on!"

As I entered the church, I saw two young men. One of them, whom I immediately recognised as a Jew, was shouting: "Jewish brethren! Let us make our way to Russia! There we shall find happiness and freedom! With the victorious Soviet Army we shall return and overthrow the Fascists!"

Bessarabia, a province which up till then had been Rumanian territory, had been occupied by the Russians, and the Jews were fleeing *en masse* because of the anti-Semitic persecution. But the government of Rumania at that time was Fascist; such talk in our church might lead to arrests. It might even result in a great many people being killed.

I tried to stop the two young men, but it was impossible. They attacked me, shouting: "You are a traitor to the Jews! You are on the side of the Fascists!" It was impossible for me to call in the police to put an end to the commotion, as that would have meant informing on the two young men, and condemning them to a certain death. So I broke up the meeting, and asked everyone to leave the premises and go home, speaking to no one on the way. They obeyed me.

Next Sunday this scene was repeated. I did not know what to do. I thought of closing the church.

During those days a Legionaire was killed in the capital. No one knew who had killed him, but the Jews were afraid that they would be accused, and that there would be reprisals.

One evening, as I was sitting at home, the two young men who had caused the disturbance in the church, came to see me. "We have something on our conscience we should like to confess to you."

"Go ahead," I said.

Then they told me that it was they who had killed the Legionaire. Involuntarily I exclaimed: "How could you commit a crime like that? Did it not occur to you that this man had a mother or a wife?" They replied: "He deserved to be killed, because he was a Fascist." I said to them: "I can understand you coming to seek advice from me if you feel oppressed by the crime you have committed. If you are proud of it, then there is nothing I can do for you. But now that you have told me what you have done, I repeat: You have commited a crime. A Fascist, too, is a man, and must be respected as such. If he is our enemy, we must repay his hatred with love, and not kill him."

Thereupon they went away.

After the Legionaires had been overthrown by General Antonescu, one of the young men, the one with the Jewish face, came again to see me.

"I must tell you how you escaped certain death," he said. "I am a young Communist who was captured by the Legion police while I was distributing illegal pamphlets. I was tortured, and to escape further ordeal I agreed to act as an *agent provocateur* for the Legionaires. The other man who was with me was one of their commissars. The idea was that he would pretend to be a Jew, and I was to go round with him, and enter the synagogues, Zionist organisations or wherever Jews were gathered together, and start pro-Communist discussions, insulting the Legionaires as much as I could. Anyone who fell for this trick, and agreed with me, would then be arrested by the Legion police and beaten. As an *agent provocateur* I came into your congregation, too, and I visited you in your home to confess to a murder which we had not committed. When I left your house, the Legion commissar exclaimed: 'I never thought I should hear a Jew say that Legionaires should be loved!'"

An answer based on Jesus's teaching that we should love our enemies had saved me from certain death. This was not the only time.

We were faced with the problem of how to get our community recognised by the Legion state authorities, because they did not respect the old authorisations. But how were we to get a new one? It was dangerous for a Jew merely to try to enter a public building in order to apply for it.

Finally, Mr. Allison and I decided to visit a priest who was a member of the Legion, and had been appointed an inspector in the Ministry of Cults. We went to his home, but did not find him there. His wife asked us to wait for him. All the time, Legionaires were coming in and out of the house, with their greeting, "Long live the Legion and its Captain!" If they had known who we were, they would have torn us to pieces.

At last the priest turned up. When he heard my name, which sounds German, he was very pleasant, and asked us with a great show of kindness what we wanted. Great was his surprise when I told him: "I am a Jew who believes in Jesus, and represent a congregation of similar Jews. We have come to make two requests. In the first place, we do not want any exception to be made of us when anti-Semitic measures are set on foot, whether this involves confiscation of property, deportation or death. I don't want our Christian faith to bring us any material advantage. The second is this: the synagogues are operating freely, and we too would like to have the right to exercise our form of worship without interference."

The priest, who was known for his violent nature—on one occasion, at the head of a group of Fascists, he had demolished with an axe a Baptist church in his district—burst out laughing, shaking all over with mirth. "There are no such things as Christian Jews," he said. "The old Metropolitan Pimen once baptised a Jew in the Bahlui River in winter. A hole had to be cut in the ice, and when the Metropolitan dipped the Jew for the third time in the water" (this is Greek Orthodox practice) "he slipped out of his hands, slid under the ice, and vanished. The Metropolitan exclaimed: 'This is the only Jew who has been baptised and died a Christian!' Other Jews baptise only their skins, and lead an un-Christian life. I do not believe that you are Christians, either."

I answered: "You have every right to reproach us. It is presumptuous of a man to declare that he is a Christian when it is written that whoever says that he is in Christ Jesus must live as Jesus lived. We have tried to do this, but as yet we have not made a great deal of progress. So we are not angry when other real Christians, who are Jesuses in miniature, reproach us for the mistakes we make in our lives. But we beg you to give us a chance, and we shall do our very best!"

He continued for a long time to insult and mock us, but

we answered by confessing our sinfulness humbly, and not defending ourselves. Our answer was always the same: "Yes, we are wicked, despicable hypocrites as you say we are. But we have a faith which will save us from sin. We are liars, but our faith is the true faith. Give us an opportunity to prove it!"

I remembered one of the beautiful incidents related in the Patristic writings. It was said of Father Agathon that a great many people came to see him, as he enjoyed the reputation of being a good man. Some of them tried to make him angry, saying: "Are you Avva Agathon? We have heard of you, that you are an adulterer and a man of great pride." And he answered: "That is true, that is so." And they said to him: "Are you the Agathon who speaks ill of others?" And he said: "I am." And they said again: "Are you Agathon the heretic?" And he answered: "I am not a heretic." So they begged him: "Tell us, why did you admit everything we said to you, but refuse to admit that you were a heretic?" He answered: "I admitted the first charges, as this is useful to my soul. But the word 'heretic' means separation from God, and I do not wish to be separated from Him." When they heard this, they were amazed at his integrity, and they left his presence uplifted.

Defending oneself when faced with accusations is not worthy of a Christian. Neither Joseph in the Old Testament, nor the Virgin Mary, defended themselves when they were accused of things they had not done. Hold your peace, and God will defend you! You will be defended by the future development of events.

As the priest continued to rain down insults upon us, we answered his accusations against Christian Jews by admitting that they might be true, but we defended our faith. The result was that the priest suddenly changed his threatening tone: "I have been deliberately testing you, and I have discovered that you are worthier of bearing the name of Christian than we are. I shall expect you early tomorrow morning at the Ministry, and you will get the licence to continue your work."

The next day I was received by him in his office like a brother, and was given the authorisation that I had never dreamed I should obtain.

Soon after this we lived through the bloody days when the Legionaires quarrelled with their friend General Antonescu and the Jews had to pay the bill for this.

Some people wonder whether the Devil really exists: the terrible chapters in the history of mankind are the best proof of his existence. Where a doctor diagnoses debility, subnormal temperatures, coughing, spitting, and strange noises in the lungs, he is no longer in doubt. This illness is caused by an invisible agent, the Koch microbe. And when I see misery spreading all over this world that has been blessed by God with all His good gifts, I assume the presence of an invisible agent, the Devil.

Jewish blood was a commodity of no value. Jews were collected wherever they were to be found, and taken to the woods or to the slaughterhouse and killed.

But anyhow the Legionary government was toppled, and now it was their turn to be arrested and killed. Our little Christian Jewish community was now in a position to help the families of the arrested anti-Semites. One family, in great distress, was just about to commit suicide when we managed to come to their rescue.

The Jews have often reproached us for extending our love to include the enemies of the Jews. We shall answer them with another story taken from the life of the Jews.

When the rabbi Susia from Anipole was still unknown, a Jew from the country used to visit him, bringing gifts. This Jew's prosperity grew from year to year.

On one occasion, when he returned to Anipole, he found the rabbi away from home. On enquiring where he was, he was told: "He has gone to Meserici, to visit his great master."

The Jew thought to himself: "The best thing for me to do would be to visit the famous teacher myself. Then I could receive a blessing from a greater authority than the rabbi Susia." So he made his way to Meserici, gave a gift to the teacher, and received his blessing. But from that day good luck deserted him and his house: his fortune gradually decreased, his business affairs went from bad to worse, and finally stark poverty stared him in the face.

In his distress he went to see the rabbi Susia and told him everything. The rabbi answered: "Our wise men have said that God requites on the same scale that we offer to him. You must know that as long as you made no choice, and gave help to poor Susia, God did the same to you, and He gave you riches. But as soon as you started to have preferences, and took a gift to the great man, then God too worked by preferences, and gave His help to someone who was more worthy than you."

We must not be selective in our good deeds. The enemy we have conquered must also have our help. But any help given to an enemy while he is in power is wrong, because it makes us his accomplices.

Of course we owe Christian love to everyone: as Christian Jews we must learn to show humanitarianism also to suffering and defeated anti-Semites, and to do this in deeds and not merely in empty words.

"What shall I do to be saved?"

Now, under Antonescu, another anti-Semitic government was in power. Our permit to worship, given by the Legionaires, was no longer valid. When Britain broke off diplomatic relations with Rumania, the English pastor and all the teachers had to leave. The English Church Mission was dissolved. The buildings which had belonged to the Mission had been administered by a German. He closed down the assembly hall, and ejected us from our flat.

Our little congregation, which now consisted of about one hundred adult members, was left without a shepherd who cared for a small flock of converted Jews.

The leader of the Lutheran Church was a Nazi bishop who had acquired a certain notoriety as a result of a sermon in which he declared that mankind had three great models—Jesus, Beethoven and Hitler, but that Jesus was greater than Hitler. In keeping with the ideas of his own idiotic sermon, instead of using the old greeting, "Praised be Jesus", he stuck to "Heil Hitler".

Baptists, Pentecostalists and Adventists were also persecuted.

The Greek Orthodox priests had persuaded General Antonescu to dissolve their congregations and confiscate their meeting houses, many of which were converted into dance halls and cinemas. Hundreds of brethren who belonged to these confessions were sentenced to as much as twenty years' imprisonment, and this at a time when we were told that the country was waging a holy crusade against Bolshevik atheism. The main accusation against all these religious groups was that they had become Judaised. The leaders of the Baptist congregation implored us: "Please don't come to us! If we receive a large group of Jews, we shall be still more bitterly persecuted."

Among the Greek Orthodox priests and hierarchy there were some who were my faithful friends. One priest published my articles at a time when anti-Semitism was at its peak. The Patriarch Nicodim himself intervened on our behalf. The old Archimandrite Scriban was tireless in our defence, and the same was true of others. But the bulk of the Orthodox priests were anti-Semitic. In their churches sermons were preached whose aim was to stir up the people against the Jews.

The Wandering Jew has no resting-place on earth; nor did the Christian Jews have anywhere to rest their heads within the Christian Churches. As time passed we were forced to accept this situation, and to regard anti-Semitism as a cross that would have to be borne patiently, gladly and without a murmur.

Nothing glorifies God more than bearing the Cross; besides, the Cross teaches you more than the Bible does. Thomas Münzer says that through the Cross you also learn the bitter Christ, and not only the sweet.

We could not decide what confession we should belong to. We were forced to accept the hospitality that was offered. Besides, we were not interested in denominational conflict. The Swedish and Norwegian missions to Israel, which were Lutheran, gave us their protection and their name. We were grateful for this.

And now we had to solve the problem of obtaining permission to hold meetings in our church.

I sent my visiting card to Mr. Sandu, a cabinet minister and head of the Ministry of Ecclesiastical Affairs. Thanks to my German name, I was admitted, and I started with the same approach as I had used a few months previously in my interview with the Legion priest: I expressed the hope that no exception would be made in our favour when anti-Semitic measures were set on foot, but said that until then we wanted to be allowed to practise our religion, in the same way as the Mosaic Jews were allowed to.

The Minister tried to brush me aside, suggesting that I should speak to the Director for Minority Groups, the Reverend Zenovie. I told him that I had just been to see Zenovie, but that I had not spoken to him. I had waited in his ante-room for a chance to talk to him, and I heard him send his servant to the devil because he had bought a different brand of cigarette from the one he had asked for. "He sends people to the devil, I bring them to God," I continued. "We two cannot understand one another. I do not wish to have an interview with him."

The Minister answered: "The Germans are in our country. We cannot give a permit of this kind to Jews."

I told him: "Mr. Minister, then I shall withdraw my application. We shall nevertheless continue to meet, at our own risk. But before I go I should like to tell you something. Priests of all denominations come to see you, to obtain assistance in their administrative problems. I wonder if a single one of them has spoken to you about your soul. A day will come when we shall no longer be ministers of state, clergymen, or anything else; we shall all stand naked and trembling before the Throne of God. We shall then have to answer for our deeds. Consider then what you may have to answer for, because you refused to help Christians to assemble peaceably in order to worship Jesus."

At that moment God had taken from me all my powers of reasoning, so that I completely forgot that I was a Jew, without any rights, in an anti-Semitic atmosphere, in the office of a minister of state. All he had to do would be to ring his bell, and I should have been arrested and should have vanished without a trace.

But the Lord invested my feeble words with authority. The Minister was not furious; on the contrary, I witnessed a scene which might be compared with something from the Bible. The Minister rose, and face to face with a Jew, he asked: "But what shall I do to be saved?"

I was now able to talk to him about Jesus.

From then on he was our friend and our protector. A Jew who believed in Jesus had removed a thorn of anti-Semitism from the flesh of a minister of state in an anti-Semitic government.

The famous Christian-Jewish poet, Franz Werfel, relates that in 1938 in an Austrian village the German troops collected all the Jews for deportation. With them went a Christian chaplain, who was unwilling to desert them. On the way an officer of the Brownshirts had a diabolical inspiration. He stole a cross from a churchyard and made a swastika out of it. He placed the swastika in the hands of an old rabbi, and ordered him to kiss the blasphemous symbol. The rabbi took the spurs from the cross, and gave it to the chaplain. A bullet struck the Jew who had restored the cross to its true shape.

On many occasions God used Jews for such purposes.

Now once again we had our permit; but this, too, was of short duration. Soon afterwards, together with my wife and a group of Christian Jews, I was arrested. A Rumanian woman reported to the police officer on duty, and demanded to be arrested together with the brethren of Israel. This request was granted.

When we were released, the Minister had been replaced by another, and our permit was annulled.

Underground religious activity

Within every man who has been born again there is a desire to retire from the cares and worries of external things, to calm the storm which sometimes disturbs even meditation, to achieve peace, to pass beyond the ego and to rest undisturbed on the breast of the Saviour. He desires only to remain poor, without knowing or desiring anything but his hidden God.

But we were not to be yet allowed contemplative lives of this kind: it was not until later that I could savour such joys, when I spent many years in prison.

We were now buffeted about in a tempestuous existence, without much time to strengthen the inner man. Our meetings were prohibited; we met illegally in various homes, thereby running the risk of up to twenty years' imprisonment. On occasions as many as a hundred of us gathered together in this way. We had developed the technique of secrecy.

Only on one occasion were we surprised during a meeting. The police had made the mistake of not surrounding the house, but walking through the yard and knocking at the door. We let them wait for a while before we opened up. After we had opened the door, we delayed them in the entrance, asking them who they were, what they wanted, and insisting that they identified themselves. When they finally entered they discovered that the report they had received of an illegal meeting was false. The household consisted merely of the family. The flat was on the ground floor, and all those present had in the meantime jumped out of the window.

The police were furious: they were sure that we held our meetings, but they had no proof. But in the end they were lucky, and obtained the proof they were after.

Towards the end, our meetings, which had aroused some interest even among a number of Rumanians, were attended by a Greek Orthodox man who lived by selling poultry, which he brought from the Soviet territories occupied by our troops. His frequent journeys to this part of the country aroused the suspicion of the police, who summoned him to their headquarters one day, in order to ask him what was the purpose of his travels.

He answered: "I assume that you suspect me of espionage. But you forget the proof I have that I am engaged in trade. This is the sole purpose of my journeys. Besides, you ought to know that converted Christians do not stoop to spying. I am a convert: you have only to ask the Reverend Richard Wurmbrand, and he will confirm that I attend the meetings he holds at various houses."

The police no longer suspected espionage; but they now questioned him about our religious meetings. Our brother had let the cat out of the bag, and he was now trapped. The police cunningly concealed their real purpose, and pretended that they wanted the names of those who took part in the meetings merely to convince themselves that the trader was really a convert, and above all that he was now no longer suspected of spying. In this way they secured a great many names.

At about eleven o'clock one night, I had gone to bed and was making notes for a sermon against the war, which was then raging at its fiercest. Suddenly my wife walked into the room, with a smile on her face as usual, and said: "The police have surrounded the house!" I just had time to throw my sermon down among the pile of papers on the table by the bed. A group of policemen pushed their way into the house, and declared that I was once again under arrest.

I hastened to get dressed and leave the house, as one of our three rooms was full to the ceiling of crates containing food which was to be distributed the next day in the women's prison, where about two hundred women believers—Baptists, Pentecostalists and Adventists—were interned. (We had taken upon ourselves the task of taking aid to the imprisoned brethren, as some of the heads of the different denominations had not sufficient courage to do so, while others had not the necessary initiative to set about it. When we had approached them with the suggestion that aid of this kind should be organised, they had backed out.) If the police had found these crates, how could we have explained the situation? Helping prisoners was a serious offence. Besides, we should have had to tell them where we had obtained the money. If we had refused to say for whom the food was intended, we might have been accused of economic sabotage by hoarding food. In either case, we should have been punished. But God closed the eyes of the policemen, and they never entered the room where the food was stored. They merely collected the papers on the table, and bundled them together. They took me with them. The same evening they arrested ten other believers, including a young girl of only sixteen, who was not yet converted, but who attended our gatherings.

When we reached the police station, we met the brother who was responsible for our arrest. The thought that he was the cause of our going to prison for many years made him quite desperate. The first thing we did was to console him, and try to dispel his gloom. We succeeded, and to this very day he is one of the brethren. We told no one of his mistake. Later, I was to officiate at his marriage.

The young girl was struck by a police commissar because, when asked what her religion was, she answered: "I love the Lord Jesus, but what this religion is called, I don't know." She could not possibly have given a better answer.

The situation might have ended tragically, had not God sent a man to intervene on our behalf—the Swedish ambassador in Rumania, Patrick von Reuterswärde. He was a deeply religious man, who was always doing good. His door was always open to anyone who was in need or who was persecuted, no matter to what nation, race, class or denomination he belonged. He helped Jews who had been unjustly treated, just as he afterwards helped Germans who suffered when the situation underwent a complete change.

The Swedish Israel Mission had taken us under its protection, and in this way we had made his acquaintance. As soon as he heard that we had been arrested, he intervened on our behalf, although this meant a breach of diplomatic rules, because we were Rumanian citizens, and he really had no right to interfere. Nevertheless, his intervention proved successful.

We were also fortunate in being able to quench the policemen's thirst for bribes. We decided not to worry with pangs of conscience, because we were giving our money to bandits and blackmailers. We could not distinguish between a bandit and a policeman persecuting us for our faith and presenting us with the choice: "Money or several years in prison". Out of love of money, too, the police gave me back my papers without looking through them.

On this occasion we spent only about fourteen days in prison.

While the war was at its height, when I was being persecuted both as a Jew and as a preacher of the gospel, I was able to publish several religious books under the pseudonym of Radu Valentin. It was under this name, too, that I became known among Rumanian believers. I had stumbled on a censor who was so addicted to drink that he was even prepared to allow the publication of a book condemning alcohol, provided he received a barrel of wine for his services.

Pastor Magne Solheim and his wife

Pastor Solheim, who was head of the Norwegian Israel Mission in Galatz, was constantly being molested. The authorities would come at night and search his house. He was tireless in visiting Jews in their shops, in their homes and in their camps, preaching the gospel at the same time as he gave them consolation and physical help. Finally, the authorities closed his church.

In his zeal he was a model missionary, never losing heart because of the cool reception he received from the Jews and the lack of understanding from the Christians. His wife Cilgia, a Swiss teacher, proved a faithful helpmeet.

An army captain once said to him: "What is the point of going to the Jews to preach the gospel? They only laugh at you." Solheim answered: "When you receive an order, what do you do? Do you discuss it or do you carry it out?"—"I carry it out."—"So do I. The leader of the Christian Army, Jesus, has ordered us to preach the gospel to all mankind. I am carrying out His order. The results are not my business, but His."

His devotion made a great impression where one might have least expected it. Here, the saying of the Christian martyr Ignatius became a reality: "Christianity is not a matter of persuasion, but of greatness." Out of the clay vessel of a devoted man shines a treasure in all its beauty, and this treasure attracts others.

When Feinstein was arrested (at the time we did not know that he had been killed), we wondered how we could intervene on his behalf. Finally, we decided that we should go to the murderers to plead on behalf of their innocent victim. We would go to the German Legation. Hitler's gang ruled in Rumania, constantly inciting the people to slaughter the Jews. It was in this situation that a Christian missionary and a Jew made their way to the German Embassy to help another Jew. We were received by a certain Herr Dietrich. When he talked to Solheim, he was astonished and said: "You need a large dose of idealism to leave your wonderful country of Norway and make your way to Rumania to preach to Jewish shop-keepers who are only interested in money and pleasure." It was obvious that Solheim's plea had aroused his sincere admiration. And a miracle occurred: Hitler's faithful servant promised to do everything possible to save Feinstein's life. We were subsequently convinced at the police station in Jassy that the German Embassy had in fact phoned repeatedly with this aim. But it was too late. Feinstein was dead.

The burden placed on the shoulders of the missionary who is not himself a Jew is a heavy one. As a rule, the Jews are indifferent, or even hostile. Anti-Semites mock them; the Christian clergy are often indifferent, too. In addition, there is the deep disappointment experienced when dealing with some Christian Jews.

There were some Jews who were baptised in the vain hope that in this way they would escape persecution; these people were excellent actors but had no really deep faith. I remember a Rumanian brother once asking me to go with him to visit a number of converted Jews whom I did not know. We were very well received, and for a whole hour we talked with enthusiasm. We knelt down and we all prayed. I was extremely happy. Then the Rumanian brother, who had some business to do, rose and left us. After he had gone, they began to laugh: "The goy, the fool, he really believes we are Christians!" They were convinced that I, too, was merely acting, and so they revealed their real feelings.

Faced with people like this, one tends to lose courage, even though one understands people who consider baptism a mere formality and a means of defending themselves against anti-Semitism.

Missionaries who work among Jews constantly come across people who have been baptised out of fear, or in order to marry a Christian, or to remove from their consciousness the fact that they are Jews. We tried to counteract this tendency by constantly maintaining the Jewish character of our community, and not allowing our members to change their names.

There are also difficulties with serious converts from Judaism. The Bible declares that our people are a peculiar people: and there is something peculiar about the Jew, which leaps to the eye, and he finds it difficult to assimilate himself into another environment. He takes this special trait with him into the Church.

The message of Jesus is universal and has eternal validity. The apostle Paul says that in order to win them, he will make himself a Jew for the Jews and a Gentile for the Gentiles, but he only "makes himself" the one or the other. In actual fact he has passed into the sphere of pure truth, where there is neither Jew nor Greek. Just as mathematics is the same all over the world, so is the true religion. The difference is only in language and method. It would be impossible to instruct the child of a Bushman in the same way as a Scandinavian child.

But merely because of the fact that Jesus was born a Jew, some Christian Jews assume that they are closer to Him than their Gentile brethren, and tend to look down on other Christians and patronise them. The belief in the Jew Jesus becomes just another kind of Jewish chauvinism, which is as intolerable as all chauvinism. This often results in conflicts, hidden or open, between the Gentile missionary and certain Christian Jews. A carpenter is not nearer to Jesus than a tailor because Jesus was a carpenter, nor is a man nearer to Him than a woman because He was a male. Neither has a Jewish Christian any superiority over a Gentile, though he often claims it.

Missionary work among Jews offers little spiritual satisfaction, and quickly wears missionaries out. Nevertheless, Solheim worked at this task for thirty years, assisted by his splendid wife, and many others.

A Norwegian deaconess, Olga Olaussen, worked unobtrusively but under great difficulty in Jassy during the war. Her father, who had been a fisherman, was once thrown out of his boat during a storm. For hours he wrestled with the waves. In his distress he promised God that, if he were saved, he would dedicate his children to missionary work, and this he did. "Schwester Olga" devoted all her life to the Jews, selflessly tending the sick and bringing up orphaned children. After the murder of Feinstein she worked alone with a group of Christian girls, as all the men in the congregation had been killed. She brought up these souls in the spirit of faith.

On one single occasion during the war I was given a permit to visit her congregation on a Sunday. Here I found a small group hungry for the Word of God. Knowing that I had only a day to spend there, I preached for eleven hours, from eight in the morning till eight in the evening, with an hour's break for dinner. Throughout these eleven hours the entire congregation kept their eyes and their attention riveted on the preacher.

Having written something about Pastor Solheim and Schwester Olga, who belong to the Norwegian Israel Mission, it might be of interest to describe how this Mission came into being.

During the first half of the nineteenth century, the Norwegian Lutheran Church made great efforts to spread the gospel among the heathen. One day a Christian lady asked her pastor: "Do you not think the time is now ripe to start the special task of spreading the gospel among the Jews?" The pastor replied: "No. According to the Bible it is now the time of the heathen. Israel has been rejected." The answer brought the lady to the verge of tears, but she held her peace, and bided her time.

A few months later she approached the pastor once again. "I would like to have your advice. A relation of mine had an only son. But he behaved so badly that finally the parents had no option but to send him away from home. To console them in their unhappy old age, they adopted a boy, giving him everything their own child had enjoyed, and making him heir to their possessions, even though blood is undoubtedly thicker than water. They treasured a picture of the child who had been born to them, constantly remembering him and shedding tears at night in their longing for him. The adopted child grew bold, and as time went on he started to abuse his foster-parents: "I don't want to see the picture of the other boy on the wall! How dare you mention his name? I don't want to hear you pining for him."

At this juncture the indignant clergyman interrupted the good lady's story: "He is an impudent boy, and does not deserve to stay in the house. They should send him away!"

Then the woman said: "Is not Israel the genuine son of the Heavenly Father? He was driven from home because he had been disobedient, and we, the other peoples, were adopted in his place. But God's heart is still fixed on Israel. Heaven, too, sighs for him. Is it right that we, the branches, should consider ourselves greater than the trunk, and refuse the Jews salvation?"

The clergyman now admitted his sin, and became the founder of the Norwegian Israel Mission.

For many decades now this mission has carried out work of great blessing in several Rumanian towns.

Difficulties of our position

The Jews suffered so greatly during the war, that had we followed our feelings only, we should have done nothing but embrace them and console them. God helped us to do something to assist the Mosaic Jews who were deported to Transnistria. Through our Rumanian brothers we sometimes succeded in abducting some of the Jewish children from the ghettoes, and restoring them to their parents.

But we could not be satisfied with this. The prophet Jeremiah lived during the violent attacks of the Babylonians which marked the beginning of the destruction of the Jewish state, and at that time he blamed the Jews for their sins. Jesus, called by some a new Jeremiah, did the same at a time when the Jews were suffering under the unjust rule of the Romans. Both were considered by their contemporaries to be traitors to their people.

In the writing known as *Baba Metzia*, the Babylonian Talmud accuses the prophets of sinning in their reproaches of Israel. The *Shir Raba* states that Moses, Isaiah and Elijah were punished by God for accusing Israel before the face of the Lord. Christians think the prophets were right.

We were in the same situation as the prophets of old. Despair, cruel servility and their terrible sufferings turned the hearts of the Jews to stone. Constantly the cry went up: "Let God choose another people. We are tired of being His nation!" On the other hand, the small group of Christian Jews was convinced of the truth of Jesus's saying that salvation must come from the Jews, that the Jews have a task to fulfil and that they are obliged to fulfil it.

The Jews could not understand why we should make them, the victims of the Fascists, co-responsible for all the evil that was taking place in the world, in this way apparently joining forces with their accusers and persecutors.

Our reasoning was simple. As far back as four thousand years ago the Jews were given the Ten Commandments, the basis of morality. It was revealed to them that God is One, and that God demanded from mankind a brotherhood of free men and women, a community guided by love and truth. He also promised a Messiah who would ultimately establish such a kingdom. The Jews were the people chosen by God to bring this revelation to all peoples. God endowed them with the qualities necessary to carry out their mission.

Almost two thousand years after Moses, the world still had not heard of this revelation. Julius Caesar wrote in his *De Bello Gallico* that the Gauls, the ancestors of the modern Frenchmen, still drank wine from the skulls of their conquered enemies. The Teutons and the Slavs, too, were savages at that time.

Today, the Jews form only 0.33 per cent of the world's population, yet they hold key positions in the economic, political, scientific and cultural life of a great many countries. The position of the Jews in these fields of influence is out of all proportion to their actual numbers.

This is a heavy responsibility for the Jews.

If the teacher fails to carry out his duty, and his pupils are hooligans, even going so far as to ill-treat their own teacher, who then is responsible—the pupils or the teacher? On countless occasions I have seen both Rumanians and Germans open up their hearts when Jews talked to them of the love of Jesus. Often, this has quite disarmed their anti-Semitism. When a Jew accepts the solemn task that God has given him, of being a light and of bringing this light to the nations, this generally produces a profound effect.

But Jews are not assuming this task: on the contrary, I know from my own experience how often some Jews have done their best to undermine the Christian faith. When the man who has lost his faith in Christ and His teaching of love strikes a Jew, we are sorry for the victim, but we cannot absolve him from his guilt.

We had converted a Greenshirt, an anti-Semite, who was a chauffeur by trade. This man, overjoyed at the treasure he had found in Jesus, went to the great Jewish industrialist, Goldenberg, by whom he was employed, and told him of his experience, and about the Saviour, and asked Goldenberg to accept Him. Goldenberg made fun of him: "How silly you are, Augustin! All this is nonsense. The important thing is to live, to have money, to drink, to enjoy life with women, because on the other side there is nothing."

Goldenberg was a shrewd man, who had succeeded in life. Augustin was a simple country lad. The result was that Goldenberg's words plucked the tender plant from Augustin's soul. Many Goldenbergs have worked in the same way, through the medium of newspapers, magazines, books, lectures, and through their influence in political and economic life. Is it surprising, then, that men like Augustin should return to the tavern and, inspired by the example Goldenberg has given them, try to lay their hands on money? And how are they to get hold of money, except by knocking Goldenberg on the head?

And when Goldenberg suffered, like anyone who suffers greatly, he was not prepared to listen to sermons of reproach, but we were forced to show him his guilt.

It was a divine miracle that among those who were struck down by the anti-Semitic tyranny and who were in great distress, there were some who received faith in Christ. To all outward appearance they were wretched, degraded, reduced to depths of squalor, yet they were people who had discovered the great mission of the Jews. They had accepted Jesus as the King of the Jews, King of the people whose mission in life it was to spread the Light of God through the world. These Jews regretted the years they had wasted by failing to do their duty, and now joyfully witnessed to their new faith, together with their brethren—Rumanians, Hungarians and Germans— who with them had become the spiritual Israel.

The Jewish people are not the only chosen people. God has given many people special vocations. The Indian people have given the world the highest metaphysics, whose influence can be recognised even in the Bible. The Roman people were chosen to give justice to the whole world. Even today, the leading minds in matters of law, such as Lombroso, Enrico Ferri and Pendi are Italians. All over the world, wherever justice reigns, Roman law is supreme. Wherever Roman law does not exist, injustice rears its head. The Greeks were chosen to give the world philosophy. It is said that since the death of the great Greek thinkers no new ideas have emerged in philosophy, but instead men have ruminated, again and again, on the wisdom of the ancient Greeks. The Germans and Italians have given the world great music; the Germans and Anglo-Saxons have given us modern technology. The Swiss have been chosen by God to show the world how different nations, who are enemies in other parts of the world, can live together in harmony. The British were chosen to begin all the big missionary enterprises and to give the Bible to all nations.

It is the duty of every nation to discover its special mission.

But the Jews have not remained faithful to their vocation. They have rejected, and still reject, their Messiah, who has been proved by history to be the person who has fulfilled to perfection the mission entrusted to the Jews, to be a light to lighten the world.

The Jews having failed in their spiritual mission, the task they should have fulfilled has been left to others. According to the prophecies of Jesus, the vineyard has been handed over to another people. From every nation, those who walk in the footsteps of Abraham, Isaac, Jacob, Moses, the prophets and Jesus, constitute the spiritual Israel. They have taken over our neglected inheritance, and are now spreading the light throughout the world. In this chosen band, this royal priesthood, this international brotherhood of love, there are also a number of followers of Jesus from among the Jewish people.

During the bitter war years we could not make many converts. Nor were we surprised that the Jews, who were oppressed, hounded, starved and dogged by death at every step, should not have opened their hearts to the gospel, just as we are not surprised that the lame man cannot dance and the dead man cannot move. We thanked God silently whenever He occasionally performed a miracle and a Jew, overcoming all inner and outward impediments, embraced the faith.

We did not ask too much of the new converts: we did not ask that they should walk in a new way, and deny all they had believed in up till then. After all, the Jewish religion has values which cannot be rejected; and we did not expect them to become model Christians overnight. The fish in lakes needed thousands of years to effect the transformation from salt-water to fresh-water creatures. A human being is equally incapable of changing in a few weeks, even in a few years. We had to be patient with our new converts. We were not afraid when we saw what a small grain of faith some of them had, provided this faith clung to the Great Saviour, because we knew that He who had planted the good seed would make it grow until His coming.

The converts did not come from celebrated circles of Judaism; but nor did Jesus gather His apostles from among the highest in the land. Mary Magdalene was a prostitute. We too had women of this kind. Matthew and Zacchaeus were embezzlers and traitors to their people. Saul of Tarsus had committed murder. Most of the apostles were unlettered artisans.

We did not consider that a person's past, however degraded it might have been, had any significance. God judges a man as he is at this particular moment. The only important thing to us was whether a man believed in Jesus's blood and suffering, whether he loved Him, whether he wished to be saved through Him, whether from now on he would follow Him.

It was not only Jesus's right hand, the one He stretched

out to the relatively good, pure, people which was pierced, but also His left hand, the one He stretched out to all those who were degraded, the pariahs.

We recalled one of the sayings of Meister Eckhardt: "Everyone is most concerned to remove what disgusts him most. The greater and more hideous our sins are, the more quickly and with the greater love does God forgive them, because he is greatly repelled." Many people who were burdened with great crimes received consolation, and we set their feet on the right path with thoughts such as these.

We did not as a rule have long conversations with people. We proclaimed the truth, we did not discuss it. We revealed a truth which fundamentally all of us carry inside us without knowing it, because the human soul is Christian by nature. We spoke to the conscience, not to the understanding. Those who had been chosen from the beginning to be saved, came to us. What was obvious to everyone was that they had been anointed with the oil of joy, above all other Jews.

I remember the day when the decision to confiscate Jewish house property was published. In the Mosaic families affected by this order there was great sorrow. Our brethren in the faith sang and rejoiced, for they knew that in heaven they had a better treasure which no one could take from them.

Two old people

One day my wife and I went for a walk. Hardly had we gone a few steps before my wife noticed an old Jew on the other side of the street. An Orthodox Jew by outward appearance, he shuffled along, walking with difficulty. My wife said to me: "That man has not long to live. Go and speak to him about the Saviour! I shall return home. We can go for a walk later."

I crossed over to the other pavement, and approached the old man with the request: "Would you please tell me what portion of the Law of Moses will be read in the synagogue next Saturday?" He told me, and then asked: "Do you believe in Jesus?" I answered, a little surprised: "Yes. Why do you ask?"—"Because I realise that you were looking for an opportunity of speaking to me. Young Jews don't stop people to put

questions of that sort. How old are you?"—"About thirty," I
told him. "You are young. I have believed in Jesus for forty
years, and I have spent just as many years in Satan's prison."

His answer left me speechless. We exchanged addresses, and
I promised to go to visit the old man. And what was the story
I subsequently heard?

This man, a tinsmith, had heard the gospel preached forty
years ago in the Anglican Mission, and he had believed in
Jesus. Ever since that day he had pored over his Bible, which
he knew better than I did, and had led a regular life of prayer.
But he had not confessed his faith to anyone, nor had he
been baptised, for fear that he might lose his customers, most
of whom were Jews.

The years went by, and he stubbornly refused to heed the
advice of those who urged him to side openly with Jesus, in
whom he believed in secret.

The devil rewarded him, as only the devil can: to secure
his livelihood he had refused to be baptised, and in his old
age he was reduced to beggary. Once again he was unable to
bear witness to his faith, lest he should be forbidden to ask
for alms from his fellow Jews outside the synagogue.

That was the position when I ran into him. For many
months I struggled with this man, who believed that the
Bible was the inspired word of God, and I asked him to bear
in mind the words of the Epistle to the Romans: "If thou
shalt confess with thy mouth the Lord Jesus . . . thou shalt
be saved." (Rom. 10.9). He knelt with me, we prayed together,
but he always had the same reply on his lips: "Where shall
I get my food if the Jews discover that I believe in Jesus?"
All around us were Christian Jews who had publicly confessed
their faith, and he realised that we all made a living, but the
devil had persuaded him that baptism for him would mean
starving to death.

I never ceased insisting that he should allow himself to be
baptised. Finally he came to see me, and said: "I have made
up my mind. Next week the great autumn festival starts, the
new year, and the Festival of Atonement. The synagogue will
be visited by a great many rich people who otherwise never

come near it. I shall get a great deal of money. And then I can be baptised."

I asked him how much money he expected to get, and he told me about five hundred lei, which was a lot of money for a beggar.

I continued to question him: "Do you believe that God created heaven and earth?"—"I do."—"Do you believe that God gave the Jews in the wilderness manna from heaven and water from the rock?"—"I do."—"Do you believe that Jesus fed thousands of people with a few loaves and fishes?"—"I do."—"Do you believe that Jesus can give you five hundred lei, so that you no longer need to postpone the fulfilment of God's commandment?"—"How can Jesus get the money for me? I must put off being baptised until after the religious festivals."

Without thinking, I said something which caught me unawares: "God will not receive you after the festivals are over. For forty years now you have bargained with Him, and now you let Him wait for a mere five hundred lei. God is a great God, and He will not allow Himself to be mocked. You will be received by Him today, or never."

When he left me the old man was angry, because he thought I had spoken harshly to him.

The day after the Day of Atonement, the old man's daughter came to ask me to go to him immediately at his house. He had been standing outside the synagogue in the cold autumn rain, and was stricken with double pneumonia. I ran as fast as I could, but it was too late: when I arrived he was already at the point of death. I went to find a doctor and asked him to restore the old man to consciousness, if only for a few seconds, so that he could express the wish to be baptised. But it was impossible. He died without receiving baptism.

It was my fault, too. At that time I did not know that in such a case as this, the dying man could have been baptised, on the assumption that he was a believer. The mere fact that he had sent for me in his last hour was significant.

I knew another case involving a Jew who in his younger days had heard the Word in Jerusalem, and had accepted the faith. Later he came to Rumania. Every time the question of baptism was broached he postponed the idea, declaring that he wished to be baptised in the Jordan. Several decades passed before he was able to make the journey. In his old age he finally set off on his pilgrimage to the Holy Land. He died on the way, in Istanbul, before his wish could be fulfilled. His daughter, who was also a believer, told me this with tears in her eyes, but she did just what her father had done. She was converted thirty years ago, but has still not been baptised. The young learn nothing from the old.

Horshani was the direct opposite of the old man whose story I related above. Horshani had served the synagogue all his life. He was now ninety-one, and had been pensioned off. Once a month he used to visit the members of his former congregation, and all of them would give him small gifts.

One day he went to see a man who had a young daughter, who was a fervent believer. She gave him a New Testament. His joy was indescribable. Despite his advanced age his mind was perfectly clear. He recognised in Jesus, of whom he read in the book, the Messiah for whose coming he had prayed all his life.

I went to visit him, but there was little for us to talk about: with all his heart he believed simply through reading the book.

Not long afterwards, he started dreaming dreams in which, night after night, he saw two people clad in white who advised him to make haste, because his days were numbered.

One day, during the bitter winter of 1941, he made his way with great difficulty to my home. I was surprised to see him. "What brings you here, Grandfather?"—"I've come to be baptised."

Neither the girl nor I had ever spoken to him about this. The decision was his alone.

At his age, prolonged baptismal instruction was out of the question. Nevertheless, I wanted to know what was passing in his heart, and so I asked him: "Why do you wish to be baptised?"—"Because Jesus commanded it," was his prompt reply. In order to test him, I asked again: "And why do you feel compelled to fulfil the commandments of Jesus?" He was very angry: "Fiddlesticks! Jesus is the Son of God and we must all obey Him."

I continued to question him: "Have you told your family that you are going to be baptised?" (His children were dead, and he was cared for by his grandchildren.) "Yes," he replied. "And what does your granddaughter say?"—"She said she would throw me out of the house."—"What would you do at your age? If she really throws you out of the house, you will not be able to fend for yourself."—"I shall stand out in the snow in the street with Jesus, but all the same I shall fulfil His commandment."

The old man had passed his examination with flying colours. I at once made all necessary preparations for the ceremony. A young Christian Jewess, who up till now had hesitated to take the step, happened to be in our house at the time. She also decided to be baptised when she heard old Horshani's answer, and I baptised both of them.

Thanks to the intervention of neighbours, his granddaughter did not throw her old grandfather out that very evening, but the next day he had to leave. He did not sleep on the street for a single night. God, who had given manna to the Jews in the desert, also took care of Horshani.

I procured him a Bible with large print, so that he could continue his reading. Whenever I went to see him, I would find him with either the Bible or a hymn book in his hand. As he could only walk a short distance, he was unable to attend our services, and so he did not know our hymn tunes. But this did not bother him. He sang the hymns to tunes he knew from the synagogue.

Horshani was an enthusiastic witness for his Lord, and was constantly telling others of his belief. He lived for another two years. In the end, his granddaughter took him back into her house, out of respect for the neighbours, but she treated him badly. He did not care. He often used to tell us how he saw heaven in his dreams.

One evening a neighbour came to tell us that Horshani was dying. Sister Olga and I immediately went to the house.

In a corner of the room where the dying man lay stood a cantor, who had been hired by the family, saying in his name the *Vidui*, a special formula of recantation of faith for Hebrew Christians. But Horshani's last words were: "The Lord Jesus is good; I am going to the Lord Jesus."

Antonescu's government had decreed that all Jews, even those who were Christians, should be buried in the Mosaic cemeteries, presumably in order to prevent the dead being racially corrupted. And in the Mosaic cemetery the administration would not allow Christian funeral services to be held, out of deference to the finer feelings of the Mosaic dead. During this period we were allowed to bury neither Horshani nor any other Christian Jews. Cantors sang beside their graves, but their souls were already with the Saviour, whom the cantors did not know.

5

ADDING TO THE CHURCH

The gambler and the police informer

WHEN HE WAS in prison, Oscar Wilde wrote that if Jesus had said nothing but "Her sins, which are many, are forgiven; for she loved much" (Luke 7.47) and "He that is without sin among you, let him first cast a stone" (John 8.7), then this would have been sufficient for us to believe that He was God, for these words express thoughts so lofty that no human spirit could have conceived them.

Another of Jesus's outstanding sayings is: "The Son of man is come to seek and to save that which was lost." (Luke 19.10).

Wherever we came across a repellent sin, we did not sit in judgement. We considered how we might cure the disease. A good tailor never throws away a scrap of cloth. Society must not reject people merely because they have fallen. It might be society's fault, too.

One day a young girl who was a Christian came to me in tears to tell me that her father, an inveterate card-player, had stolen her mother's money, which she had scraped together by working long hours as a dressmaker, and had gone out to gamble the money away in some inn, which one she did not know. We systematically visited all the inns in our part of town. At last, very late, we ran him to earth in a tavern which was also involved in a smuggling racket. He was absorbed in a game, and after he had lost, I tapped him on the shoulder and told him I wanted a word with him. We went into an adjoining room, and sat down at a table, the three of us—the gambler, the girl and myself. I spoke amicably, I spoke harshly; every approach was fruitless. I talked about humanity, I talked about religion.

There was one single thought in his head: he would go on gambling, to try to win back the money he had lost. In vain I argued that in these games the only person who came out the winner was the innkeeper. I told him I was resolved not to leave the inn until he agreed to come with me. He now grew insolent, and started to shout: "What rights have you over me? I am a Jew. Let the chief rabbi come to fetch me. I am not a member of your congregation, and I must ask you not to interfere in my life." He shouted so loudly that all the other cardplayers heard it, and they too began to threaten me.

I said: "Do you want the chief rabbi? I'll go and fetch him."

His daughter and I stopped the first taxi we could find and drove to the home of the chief rabbi, but he was not in town. So we went to the house of another leading rabbi, and rang the bell. After a long wait a sleepy servant opened the door. I said to him: "Please wake the rabbi, as a great misfortune has befallen Israel."

This took place at a time when anti-Semitism was raging. The servant imagined that I had come with news of some new law against the Jews. I assured him that the matter was very important.

A few moments later we were ushered into the rabbi's bedroom. He was sitting up in bed, waiting anxiously to hear what had happened. I told him of the great tragedy, that a sheep from the chosen flock of Israel was losing money, as well as endangering the sacred prestige of the Jewish race in the inn, and that he had demanded that a rabbi should come and fetch him. "There's a car waiting outside. Please come with me."

The rabbi looked at me as though I were mad. "Have you woken me up only for this? Tell the gambler that he can come and see me tomorrow, and I will talk to him." I answered: "It is not for the lost sheep to come to the shepherd. The shepherd must seek out the lost sheep. The gambling dens, the taverns and the brothels are full not only of Rumanians, but also of Jews. I visit these places to look for lost souls, but I never meet any rabbis there. Nor for that matter do I find any Christian clergymen. Do your duty as a shepherd and come with me!" He muttered a few derisory words, and rolled over in bed to go to sleep.

The girl and I returned to the inn, which was in the Jewish quarter, and told the gamblers, many of them Jews, what had happened. This gave me an opportunity of speaking to them of the Saviour, who left the ninety-nine sheep in the fold in order to look for the one which was lost. I pleaded with them to cross the gulf which a heedless priesthood of all religions had placed between Jewry and Jesus.

The gambler went back to his family. And the news of what had happened that night was talked of in all the inns.

On my wanderings into the world of the outcasts I ran into Farcash. He was a Hungarian Jew, whose name means "wolf", and he was a wolf by profession, a paid informer. He went round among the Jews, worming out of them how much foreign currency, gold or other valuables they had hidden away. With this information he went to the police commissioner, with whom he had an arrangement. The police would arrest the guilty man, and extort his gold from him by threats and torture. He would then be released, and Farcash and the policeman would split the loot between them.

Farcash's wife was a believer, and she was stricken with grief at her husband's misdeeds. At her request several of the brothers spoke with him, but he merely listened without responding.

But the seed was not lost. One day Farcash said to his wife: "Get a bath ready for me. I want to clean myself outwardly and inwardly, and become a new man."

He took a bath, and then he went to the police commissioner, and told him: "I have been born anew. I deeply regret the wrong we have done together, and I have decided to have nothing more to do with it." The result was that the police commissioner had him interned in a concentration camp at Tirgul-Jiu, for fear that he himself would be exposed.

Every third month a commission visited the camp in order to interview the internees. Farcash was one of those brought before the commission. He reported with a Bible in his hand, told them of his former life, and confessed his new faith. One police inspector grabbed the Bible and flung it to the ground. Farcash told him: "You have brought misfortune on yourself by mocking this book. Now all the curses mentioned in it will fall upon you." His fate was now apparently sealed. He had forfeited any chance of release.

But that evening the commandant, touring the camp, chanced to peep into Farcash's cell, and saw him kneeling in prayer. Out of curiosity he opened the door, and asked him who he was. Farcash told his whole story, concealing nothing. The commandant was so impressed that he promised to intervene on his behalf, and shortly afterwards he was set free.

The policeman who had torn the Bible from his hand later suffered many years of imprisonment under the Communists. Farcash was baptised. Soon afterwards he made his way to Hungary, where he was probably killed by the Nazis.

The struggle for a soul

Mrs. S. had decided for Christ, but her husband was violently opposed to her conversion. Finally, he forced her to accompany him to a rabbi, so that she could be shown the error of her ways.

She told me the time of her appointment, and I walked up and down in front of the synagogue, praying. I was afraid that the joint exertions of the rabbi and the husband would weaken her decision.

I kept it up for a while: finally I could stand it no longer, and burst into the rabbi's office. I told him who I was, and insisted that the interview with the lady should take place in my presence.

I am tall and of an athletic build; the rabbi was small and thin. He was clearly nervous. He offered me a chair, and then went on to address the lady: "Christianity is the opposite of the great message of the revelation 'Hear, O Israel, the Lord thy God is one God'. If God is one, the Father, where do we get the other gods, Christ and the Holy Spirit?"

I intervened in the discussion: "Rabbi, this assertion that

God is one is part of the mystique of numbers. It contradicts the assertions of the dualists that God is two, and of the polytheists that there are many gods. If God is identical with the number one, He must have qualities in common with this number. This shows how useful mathematics is to an understanding of the divine truths. All the philosophers, from Plato and Pythagoras to Augustine and Boethius, have maintained that no man who is ignorant of mathematics is capable of understanding divine things.

"You persist in maintaining that God is one, without realising what the term 'one' involves. There is no such thing as absolute one. 'One' simply represents a synthesis of conflicting forces. Man is one because he is a synthesis of body, soul and spirit. These again are syntheses of other entities. An atom is a synthesis of conflicting elementary particles.

"You talk about the oneness of God. But the Mosaic faith is based on a misunderstanding of the Bible meaning. The Hebrew language has two expressions for the word 'one': *iahid*, which means 'absolute unity'; and *ehad*, which means composite unity, as in the book of Genesis, Chapter 1; '*vaihi erev vaihi boker, iom ehad*—and it was evening, and it was morning, the first day, one day.'

"In the Bible, God is called *Ehad*, a composite unit. In his thirteen articles of faith, Maimonides jumped from *Ehad* to *Iahid* without any support from the Bible. It is in his work that for the first time we find God portrayed as an absolute unit, which is absurd from both a mathematical and a philosophical point of view.

"We might say that the confession of faith which thousands of Jewish martyrs had on their lips at the moment of their death should, correctly translated, run as follows: 'Hear, O Israel, Jehovah our gods'—*Eloheinu* is a plural word—'I am Jehovah of a composite unity'. Can you deny this, Rabbi?"

The rabbi was downright astounded. Although he was a very well-read man, he had no acquaintance with Christian apologetics, applied to the Mosaic faith. At this moment his intellectual curiosity gained the upper hand: "What you are saying is new and very interesting to me. Please go on!"

Mrs. S. glanced in triumph at her confused and shamefaced husband.

I continued: "If I maintain that God is one, I maintain that He is divisible, because the number one is divisible. He can be the Father, the Son and the Holy Spirit. Even the words of Jesus which he addressed to men and women, quoting from the Psalms, 'Ye are gods' (John 10.34), are plausible. All God's children share His divine nature. The number one is also capable of being multiplied. But it is unlike all other numbers because, however much one multiplies it by itself, it always remains one. We men and women, too, are made gods, but God remains one. Likewise, the number one is the only number whose square root is equal to itself. That is why Jesus, a man, was able to say: "He that hath seen me hath seen the Father" (John 14.9). That is why we have retained the saying used by the early Christians: 'Every time you look at a brother, you look at God.'

"God has been called one because every number is a quantity related to one. In this way the whole creation is related to God. At any rate, you cannot use the fact that God is one as an argument against the Christian faith."

In the rabbi's office there was only one picture—a reproduction of "The Last Supper" by Leonardo da Vinci. Why precisely *this* work of art? I put the question straight to the rabbi.

Somewhat shamefacedly, he answered: "I admire Jesus because He was a great Jew, just as I admire Plato, the great Greek. They were both important thinkers and good men. I also believe that we should bring back Jesus to the ancestral heritage of the Jewish nation. But if Jesus had been asked what His religion was, He would have answered: 'The Mosaic faith'. Jesus was a Jew, not a Christian. I have nothing against this lady loving Jesus, but that love should be an extra stimulus to help her to remain wholeheartedly what Jesus was too, a Mosaic Jew."

I answered: "Since you have mentioned Plato, I think we had better remain in the pure sphere of philosophy. In heathen religions, divinity could not be worshipped in any other way than according to concepts which people hold about its very nature. But the Christian and the Mosaic cults, too, are in danger of degenerating into idolatry if we attribute to the divine an image that springs from our own understanding. So let us move from cult to philosophy, from images to the final realities!

"As a rule, we do not draw conclusions from what we say ourselves. You tell me that you admire Plato, probably for his teaching. But if you consider this teaching correct, why do you not adopt it?

"Platonism had many of the ideas of Christianity before the time of Christ. Plato demonstrated the philosophical necessity for a *logos* as an intermediary between God and man. He called it *Nus*. No cause can produce an effect which is not related to it. The Invisible God could not simply produce the visible world. What first emanated from Him was the invisible idea which, because it contained within itself, in an ideal manner, everything that can exist as a reality, and because it was essentially active, created the universe."

The rabbi answered: "The idea of a *logos* is acceptable to us also; it is not especially Christian. We have it from Philo of Alexandria. But the *logos* is not God. You say that it was born of the Father; if it was born, then it cannot have existed before its birth. It is not eternal, therefore it is not God. God is only one. Perhaps Jesus will come to be appreciated and recognised as one of the great prophets of Israel. Perhaps our judgement of Him will be revised. But we shall never accept the Trinity."

I explained our position to him: "The Word was born logically, not chronologically, from the Father. He is eternal. And the word 'Trinity' ought not to shock you. When we talk of divinity, our words are inadequate. Human language is the result of men's need to understand one another in their working, family and social lives. How could we have words for the metaphysical realities? Even Christians use the word 'Trinity' with a certain amount of reserve. As Augustine said, when you start to count the Trinity, you abandon the truth. And Luther, who constantly used the expression 'The Holy

Trinity', wrote: 'The name "The Holy Trinity" is not to be found anywhere in the Scriptures, but has been invented by men. For that reason it has a cold ring about it, and it would be better to say God than Trinity . . . There exists a Being of divine nature; the strongest union between body and soul is not as united as God is united . . . Not only do we believe in and learn about a unique God, but a God of the simplest simplicity and the most united unity.'

"On the other hand, even the Old Testament has been unable to avoid the figure three, which is the measure of everything. Here, too, we read of the Son, for example in Psalm 2: 'Kiss the Son, lest he be angry, and ye perish from the way,' or in Isaiah, Chapter 9, where we read of a child who is to be born, whose name is to be the Mighty God. And there are countless passages which speak of the Spirit of God. Virgil wrote: 'the unpaired delights the Divinity'. In God we must look for the source of everything, for the means by which He receives again what He has created, and for His purpose, which is sanctification and perfection. In order to describe God in human words we need the term 'Trinity'."

The rabbi cut me short: "Holiness means being faithful to the past, to a treasure which was entrusted to Israel several thousands of years ago. God appeared to Moses as one; everything else is human speculation.

"Madam," he went on, turning to the lady, "I cannot recommend that you should follow the adventurous road of the Christians. Remain on the ancient rock of Mosaic belief!"

Mrs. S. and her husband, both of them intelligent people, had attentively followed the discussion without speaking. Now that she had an opportunity to speak, the woman gave the conversation an entirely different twist, as she said to the rabbi: "You are speaking against the Christian faith. You advise me not to embrace it. Rabbi, do you wish Christianity to disappear? Do you realise what a catastrophe would overwhelm the world if it were to contain nothing but Hitlerism, Communism, and terrible suffering? What would be left of the world, what would become of Jewry without the thousands of converted people among the Gentiles who, out of love for

Christ, spread love around, and spread what the Jews neglect to spread—the Jewish Bible, the Revelation given to us by God so that we in turn might give it to other nations? There is no alternative to Christianity, because the Mosaic faith is nationally isolated. In fact, it is passive within the Jewish race also. The Mosaic faith cannot give light. Moses was made known in the world because of Jesus. I ask you once again, Rabbi, do you want Christianity to disappear?"

The rabbi made a deprecatory gesture, and exclaimed: "God forbid!"

"Well," continued the woman, "if you want it to survive, and if you want it to survive as the religion of perfect love, then you must want Jews to be converted to it. Because the Church of Christ needs Jews, just as lungs need air. And we, the Jews, need Jesus, our King. Just as a swarm of bees, separated from the queen, loses its sense of direction, so we have lost our sense of direction without Him. I wish to become a Christian."

The rabbi turned to her husband: "Let her have her way! I can do no more."

As we left, I said to the rabbi: "What you and I said about God might seem contradictory, but any statement about God is fraught with danger, because we attribute to Him human concepts. We find God only on the *via negationis*, the way of negation, by denying what the human imagination has woven around Him. We are on opposite sides, but let us both know God as the place where opposites meet. In Him, in Him alone, because He is eternal, the difference between a straight line, a triangle and a circle vanishes. In infinity all geometrical shapes are alike, and religious differences disappear. Only love unites the lover with the beloved. The more men love and understand one another, the more they acquire of the Divine Being. When we reach the heights where love dwells, we find that the King in the kingdom of love, He who showed us this road in the most sublime way, and who Himself suffered death for love of His creatures, is Jesus."

The rabbi was friendliness itself when he shook hands with us and we departed, leaving him alone in his office to gaze at the picture of the Last Supper. Shortly afterwards, the woman was baptised.

A soul lost and a soul found

A gentleman came to see me, introducing himself by a Rumanian name. He said he was on the verge of suicide: I was the last person whose advice he was seeking before taking his life.

He told me his sad story. He was a Jew, who had been baptised twenty years previously, without a shred of belief. He had merely wished to escape the sorry fate of being a Jew. He had joined the Greek Orthodox Church, had adopted a Rumanian name and married a Rumanian lady. He had been lucky up to now.

The anti-Semitic government now in power was not interested in a man's religion, but in his race. When they discovered that our friend was born a Jew, his house was confiscated, and he was expelled from the Law Association of which he was a member. When he lost his source of livelihood, his wife and his Rumanian friends abandoned him. He had long been a stranger to the Jews. Now he was desperate and unhappy.

I told him that I had a very influential friend whom we could consult immediately. I was certain that this friend would help him. He thanked me warmly, and assured me that he would repay me handsomely. Great was his disappointment when I told him that my friend was Jesus Christ, and suggested that we should kneel together and speak with Him.

"But how can anyone talk to Jesus? He died two thousand years ago."

"Don't you believe that He has risen from the dead?"—"No."—"Don't you greet your friends every Easter, as is the Greek Orthodox custom, with the words 'Christ is risen'?"—"Yes."—"Then if Christ is not risen, you are a dishonest man, because every year, when in answer to this greeting you declare, 'He is risen indeed', you are telling a gross lie. You must decide: either He is in truth risen, or you are a patent liar. If you believe neither the gospel nor the Church, then at any rate believe in what you have so many times declared.

Choose: either Christ is risen, or you are a base liar, a man without honour."—"Christ is risen."—"Did He die again after His resurrection?"—"No."—"Then He is alive, and we can talk to Him."—"How can He be alive?"

Three times our argument went round in a circle. Again and again he was faced with the alternative which must be faced by all who confess the Christian faith without believing: either Christ is risen, or you have been living a lie. But I could not get him to believe in Jesus Christ as a living Saviour and counsellor.

He did not commit suicide: he did something much worse.

He had done his national service as a wireless operator, and now he volunteered for the army. Although Jews were not normally accepted, his application was successful because he had been a member of the Orthodox Church for a long time, and also because he was a much-needed specialist. At the front he distinguished himself by committing atrocities against Jews and raping Jewish girls. After the fall of the Nazis, he was sentenced as a war criminal.

This should not surprise us. There were other Jews who took part in the Rumanian anti-Jewish atrocities. Mrs. Marin, who was sentenced to death after the revolt of the Legionaires, during which more than a hundred Jews were killed, was a Jewess. Every nation has its traitors. The Jews are no exception. Marx was an anti-Semitic Jew, so are some of the Communist Jews who are leaders of Rumania today, such as Leonte Răutu and Cornel Manescu.

An old Christian Jew had a shrew of a wife who hated Christian Jews with all her heart. When her husband, a poor man, wished to attend our meetings, she hid his only pair of trousers. When he left the house, she would call out through the window: "I hope you break your leg, you renegade!" Whenever he brought home a Jewish friend and testified to him of his Lord, she would interrupt: "Don't believe my husband. He has sold himself!" For years the old man had to put up with this treatment. Meanwhile, his children grew up. One of them did very well for himself, and had an important job with a foreign oil company. He loved his father, and invited him to stay for two months' holiday.

When I heard of this, I had an idea. No one had been able to talk to his wife. Several of the brethren had tried, but she would seize the first thing that came to hand and throw it at them. Now I saw an opportunity of reaching her. I asked her husband to entrust me with the task of collecting his monthly wages and taking them to his wife, who would be informed of this plan. She was in such need of money that she would have to receive me.

On the first day of the following month, I turned up. She expected me to hand over the money at the door. But I was in no hurry. I told her I was thirsty, and asked for a glass of water. In this way I managed to get into the house, where I sat down on a chair. She waited for me to hand over the money. I started to talk about the hot, dry weather we were having. I asked for another glass of water. Then I told her that I had heard of her aversion to the Christian Jews, and I quite understood her attitude. I had been one of them for several years, and I realised what a collection of sinners I had joined. She pricked up her ears. I launched into a long speech about the number of hypocrites and renegades among them, how inconsistent they were, and how their words and their deeds were poles apart. We were now on common ground. I had touched on a subject which found an echo in her heart.

She too expatiated on the sins of the Christian Jews she knew. I joined her in condemning their transgressions. We got on very well. I gave her the money. I now had access to her house, because she recognised in me a kindred spirit.

I returned several times. The first time, I merely talked to her about the wickedness of Christian Jews. The same thing happened on the second occasion. Then I added, almost as an afterthought: "Of course, we are all sinners. Have not you and I also sinned?" At each visit she had a little more opportunity of thinking about *our* sins and a little less about other people's.

After a while, I had made such good progress that I managed to persuade her to attend one of our meetings. She was very embarrassed, because she knew her reputation. But I had carefully prepared the brethren, and told then how to receive her. One of them was to give her a hymn book; another was to see that she got a seat near the window. One of the sisters would ask after her rheumatism, and would tell her that the seat near the window was no good, as there was a draught. All the young people were to greet her with great respect. She was enthusiastic when the meeting was over. Soon she was converted.

Her husband knew nothing about this. When he returned, she asked him, with tears in her eyes, for forgiveness. As he had suffered patiently for twenty years, when he heard this and knew that there was no longer any need for him to hold his peace, he gave her the scolding which he had not dared to give her in the past.

She was not dismayed; she became a loving and believing sister, and in many ways surpassed her husband.

God chooses people by whom the world does not set great store—simple souls who have stumbled, and who in their ignorance have become a prey to wickedness. Our congregation consisted mostly of simple men.

Jesus said, "I thank thee, O Father, Lord of heaven and earth, because thou hast hid these things from the wise and prudent, and hast revealed them unto babes." (Matt. 11.25). Why should this be? I believe that God is anxious that His message should not be perverted, this message which is destined to play such a great role in these days. Intellectuals are seldom capable of coveying a message just as they have received it, without giving it a personal twist; whereas the simple, ignorant people transmit it faithfully. But although there were not many intellectuals in our ranks, that does not mean that there were none at all.

Practical action

In the conditions under which we lived, our mission embraced a wide range of activities apart from our main task, which was to preach the gospel to the Jews.

When the German army occupied Rumania, we considered

it our duty, out of love for our enemy, to print a special edition of St. John's Gospel, and distribute it free to German soldiers. When they received these handouts on the streets, they admitted to our brethren that they had been prepared for quite a lot in Rumania, but they never expected to find Jews giving them the Word of God as a free gift!

When Bucharest was bombed, I started systematically preaching in air-raid shelters, thus reaching both Jews and Rumanians with the Word of God.

When the first Russian air raids took place, I and six other brethren were under arrest. We were just being interrogated when the alert sounded. We were taken to the shelter under escort of armed guards, and the judges, lawyers and members of the public joined us. When the first bombs began to fall, I suggested: "Let us all kneel, and I shall say a prayer." They all knelt, including the officers and guards. They crossed themselves as I prayed aloud. Then I preached a sermon on the necessity of being prepared to meet God. They all listened reverently.

When the all-clear sounded, the guards seized us by the collar and escorted us back to the court. Once again I stood in front of the judge who only a quarter of an hour before had knelt at my command, and answered his questions.

After we had been released, every time we heard the air-raid warnings we would run as quickly as we could to a large shelter, and preach. Once we ran with Sister Olga to a shelter in a large block of flats. Though it was forbidden to be in the streets once the warning had sounded, I was seized with a sudden impulse to leave the building and we made our way to another shelter. The house we had left was destroyed by bombs, burying a great many people in its ruins.

During another raid a sister and myself were arrested on a charge of spreading anti-war propaganda under the pretext of preaching. We were released after once again having to pay a considerable bribe.

Our activities were many-sided. One of them was to help our brothers whom the Greek Orthodox Church called sectarians. Because they were Adventists or Baptists, they were sent to prison and sometimes suffered terrible tortures. We managed to procure the intervention on their behalf of the Swedish Ambassador.

Much of our time was spent helping the Mosaic and Christian Jews who were forced to do heavy manual labour without being paid a cent. Occasionally some of them were able to scrape a bare pittance during the hours of the night. I also had to ease the conscience of our brethren in connection with this work. One of them had an illegal workshop, where he produced crates for fruit. All day long he worked, without any form of remuneration, for the state, which did not even provide him with food. How was he to provide for his five children?

One could not help admiring some of the brethren who, in these circumstances, carried out their civic duties and were unwilling to break a single one of the rules imposed by the Fascist government. But I had to explain to them that according to the Scriptures the authorities were instituted to punish evil and reward good. If they did the very opposite, then we were absolved from our duty to obey them.

Besides, all this time we were busy doing things which according to the law carried the death penalty, such as helping a number of Jews from Hungary to cross the frontier illegally, and rescuing children from ghettos.

Towards the end of the war our little community in Jassy was in danger. We were afraid that the Germans, as they retreated, would start a new pogrom. The trains were crammed with Rumanians fleeing before the approaching Russian army. Jews were not allowed to travel. An acquaintance of mine, a high-ranking military officer, arrested all the members of the community on a fictitious charge. One brother, who was a soldier and armed with a rifle, was ordered to escort the "traitors to the state" in a carriage especially reserved for them. At the railway station in Bucharest the order of arrest was torn up, and the arrested persons were handed over to the charge of my wife. Many Rumanian brethren risked their lives to help us on this occasion.

As far as courage is concerned, the Babylonian Talmud says: "The words of the Torah [the Divine Law] are only in the keeping of him who is prepared to die for their sake. For it is written in the Book of Numbers: 'This is the law, when a man dies . . .'" (Num. 19.14).

In-fighting

Jesus taught the people in the synagogues. He expects His disciples to do the same, and He warns them: "They will scourge you in their synagogues" (Matt. 10.17). This presupposes that we shall speak to the people, and annoy our listeners with sermons which intentionally attack their prejudices and superstitions.

This is precisely what we did.

It was a Friday evening: the Jews were assembling early in their synagogues to read from the Holy Book or to debate among themselves before the start of the service.

I sat down next to the rabbi and asked him, loudly so that those who were sitting near us could also hear: "Rabbi, I have been told that there is a book written by a Jewish prophet called, so far as I can remember, Isaiah. Is it a good book, worth reading?"

"What a question!" he answered. "If only you would read it! It contains nothing but pure gold."

"Rabbi, I have read a great many books where I imagined I would find valuable things, only to discover that I had been fooled. Won't that also be the case with Isaiah?"

"Young man, the very thought is a sin. In fact, it was not Isaiah but God Himself who wrote it. Isaiah was merely the pen."

"Rabbi, where can I find the Book of Isaiah?"

He fetched it down from a shelf and gave it to me. Before opening the book, I asked him again to assure me that it contained God's own words.

Then I opened it at Chapter 53, and asked him: "Rabbi, to whom does this refer?" and I read out aloud the passage describing the Suffering Servant. "This description tallies exactly with Jesus," I said. "He must be the Messiah."

The rabbi exclaimed: "You should not read that passage. You ought rather to read Chapter 11."

I turned to the Jews. "Dear friends! You have heard the rabbi confirm that every word in this book is God's own word. Then this description of Jesus's sufferings must also have been inspired by God."

The rabbi angrily left the synagogue, banging the door behind him. He thought I would be polite enough to leave too; but I let him go, and stayed behind with the Jews, explaining Isaiah's prophecy to them.

Another Friday several of our Rumanian brethren came with us to the synagogue where another celebrated rabbi was going to preach. When the service was over, one of them asked aloud: "Please tell me what the inscription on your synagogue means. I am a Rumanian, and I do not understand it." The rabbi answered: "It is a verse from the prophecies: 'My house shall be called a house of prayer for all nations.'" Our brother asked in a puzzled voice: "But if your synagogue is intended to be a house of prayer for all nations, why did you mumble in Hebrew all this evening—a language which not even the Jews can understand? Perhaps you are concealing truths which you should be giving us, too." The rabbi left the synagogue.

Then another Rumanian stood up and preached the good news of Jesus. I mingled with the Orthodox Jews, whose knowledge of Rumanian was not very good, and translated the sermon into Yiddish. We were well received, and listened to attentively.

The Bible tells us that if we behave like this we shall be scourged in the synagogues. This did not happen to us. Instead, a number of our enemies among the Jews got together and planned to scourge us in our own church.

Pastor Solheim came to Bucharest, where the Norwegian Israel Mission established a station. We had taken over and decorated the building that had formerly belonged to the Anglican Mission to the Jews, and we were now going to dedicate the church. We invited one of the leading pianists of Bucharest to play to us, and we had posters put up all over the city, inviting the Jews to come to our inaugural ceremony.

On the Sunday morning, the church, which could accommodate up to five hundred people, was crammed with Jews. One could sense that some of them had come with evil intentions, and were even organised.

Solheim preached in his usual calm way, and was listened to attentively. I seized the bull by the horns, and told the Jews what God meant when He declared through the mouth of the prophet Isaiah: "Why should ye be stricken any more?" (Isa. 1.5). Our old people had been gassed, our children burned in the furnaces. This could not happen to a people chosen by God, of whom it is written that whoever touches him, touches the apple of His eye, unless a serious conflict had arisen between him and his Creator. "In the prayer book of the synagogue the worshippers constantly repeat that sufferings have overwhelmed our people because of our sins. Turn then from the great sin of rejecting the Messiah, given to us by God in order that we might turn God's wrath from us. Listen to what is written in the Law of Moses: 'The Lord [not the Nazis] shall send upon thee cursing, vexation and rebuke, in all that thou settest thine hand unto for to do, until thou be destroyed, and until thou perish quickly; because of the wickedness of thy doings, whereby thou hast forsaken me.' (Deut. 28.20).

"The Torah tells us that the disaster which strikes us down is because of 'our wicked doings', and not the wickedness of our persecutors. Surely our refusal of Jesus, the incarnation of God, is the greatest sign of our being in error?"

The Good Samaritan bathed the wounded man's injuries with oil and wine. Solheim's task was to apply oil, to soothe pain. Mine was to bathe wounds with alcohol. One is no good without the other, but it hurts to apply wine to open wounds.

At a pre-arranged signal, shouting, whistling and a general hubbub broke out, reminding us of the passage in the Bible describing how Stephen's accusers, when they heard his witness, "gnashed on him with their teeth" (Acts 7.54). The din was terrific. A group of Jews rushed across to strike me. But my wife, having foreseen what would happen, had organised a solid phalanx beside the pulpit. They could not reach me. Pastor Solheim whispered to me delightedly. "It is good that this should happen, that the word of God has moved them. It is far worse when the audience is indifferent."

It was not the first time in the history of our mission that this sort of thing had occurred. In the days of Pastor Adeney, young Jews had smashed the windows during a service, and danced in the church. We were used to this kind of incident, and we did not lose our heads. When our brethren tried to calm them, the troublemakers leaped at them. But the brethren were not prepared to give in. One sister, a stout woman, removed her shoe and laid about her with might and main. The result was a regular rough house, which lasted for nearly two hours.

In the afternoon we had a repeat performance, and this went on for the next few Sundays, until we were forced to enlist the aid of the police, who restored order.

While all this was going on, I realised why, when the Jews stoned Stephen, someone had to look after the clothes of the murderers. It is true that they were zealous of the Law of Moses, but they would not stop at stealing a colleague's clothes, if they could. During the fighting, various articles disappeared belonging to our attackers, who came back to look for them; but in vain, as their own people had taken them.

When we were at last left to ourselves, I reproached the brethren for their violence, and reminded them of Jesus's teaching about turning the other cheek when anyone strikes you. They replied: "When anyone strikes you, yes, but when anyone strikes your pastor, then you must teach them a lesson they won't forget!"

The use of force is the touchstone which proves whether a man is in truth determined to fight for justice. On one occasion I gave two slaps to someone who was disturbing our meeting. St. Nicholas gave Arius a slap on the ear, too, and he was not angry. Now and again one must use violence for the sake of one's faith.

One Sunday I took hold of a Jew, who had long been attending our meetings but who refused to be converted, and forced him to his knees. I told him: "You won't be allowed to stand up until you have surrendered to the Lord!" He said a prayer. Twenty years have passed since this happened, and he and all his family are believers.

What gave us strength during this period of in-fighting was that at this time we were in the habit of fasting often and spending whole nights in communal prayer. In prayer, something like an echo takes place. When you strike a note on the piano, corresponding strings in all the other pianos in the room start to vibrate. It is just the same when we express a pure wish in our ardent prayers: all around us we mobilise angels who are inspired by the same wish.

Unusual phenomena

The so-called parapsychic phenomena, such as telepathy, clairvoyance, visions of various kinds, spiritualism and so on, are today objects of scientific investigation in several university faculties. It is accepted that there are means of perception other than through the senses. Through what sense did the learned Russian Lomonosov perceive, at a distance of thousands of miles, that his father had drowned, and that his body had been washed up on an island where, in fact, it was subsequently discovered?

The fact that extra-sensory perception exists explains how it is possible for the soul to survive after separation from the body. If the soul can transmit only by the physical senses, then after separation from the body it must enter a state of suspension, without pleasure and without pain, without perception, without any possibility of growth. Investigations into parapsychic phenomena have shown that this is not so, that the soul has its own sources of perception and information, since it has joys and sorrows which are not conditioned by the state of the body. After death, the soul can live an independent life.

Christians live in the world of miracles. I should like to recount some of the remarkable things that have happened to us. I know that to people who do not inhabit the same world as us, these experiences will seem impossible, but we should remember Hamlet's words: "There are more things in heaven and earth . . . than are dreamt of in your philosophy."

One winter's night I was walking home with my wife. The stars were shining with extraordinary brightness. I said: "On a night like this, when the stars are shining in the sky just as they are now, God took Abraham out of his tent and said to him: 'Look up at the sky and count the stars! I shall make your seed as numerous as the stars in heaven and the sand on the seashore.'"

We were both seized by the Spirit of God. Dumb with wonder, we ran home as fast as we could. The splendour of the promise given to our ancestor Abraham was almost more than we could bear.

We lived on the ground floor, with the windows facing the street. One night, at about two o'clock, we were both awakened by something. We both thought we had heard someone knocking on the window and shouting, and we whispered: "It sounds like Anutza," who was one of our sisters in God. But at the same time we were frightened that it might be the police. We listened. All was quiet. We went to sleep again. After a while we were awakened once again, with the same strange feeling. Once again we went to sleep. We were awakened a third time, and we both distinctly heard the words: "I love you with an eternal love."

One morning I was lying on my sofa. It was after my first imprisonment. I suffered from tuberculosis of the lungs and spine, and had to spend a great deal of time lying down. I had a terrible feeling of the presence of an invisible evil power. In my terror, I cried: "Out, out, and as a sign that you, Evil One, have been here, you shall bang the door behind you!" The door opened, and closed again slowly, untouched by human hand. I was free!

One day I was walking through one of the narrow streets of Bucharest, at about eleven in the morning, a time when the streets are crowded. Suddenly I felt an irresistible urge to take out my fountain pen and writing pad. I leaned against a post, and started to write, as though I were taking dictation. I was amazed at what I wrote. After half an hour I had com-

pleted the draft of a book, which was excellently received and
ran through three editions in Rumanian. It is called *The
Mirror of the Human Soul*, and deals with Christian psychology,
a branch of science which held no special interest for me at
that time.

An article of mine which was most favourably commented
on was *The Shepherd on the Rock of Error*, which I dreamed.
All I had to do was to write down my dream.

One night I dreamed a complete sermon on the subject
of contention among Christians. This dream proved prophetic,
as shortly afterwards our congregation was rent by a conflict.

One day, several Christians belonging to different confessions
were gathered together. My son, then about four years old,
was playing in the room. The brethren started a lively discussion on confession, contradicting one another violently.
At the height of the discussion my son, who was still playing,
called out: "*Kardia kai psyche mia*" (a phrase in ancient
Greek from the Acts of the Apostles, where the first Christians
are described as being of "one heart and one soul"). The
brethren cut short their argument and asked me what the
words meant. I explained, and the quarrel ended. The words
had come just at the right time.

I can think of only one explanation of the incident. I had
read the New Testament in Greek, and as I liked this expression, I had read it to my wife and explained it to her.
This explanation lay hidden in the subconscious of my child,
who was very interested in religion from his earliest years,
and who must have been present in the room at the time. The
amazing thing is that he should have used these words at
precisely the right moment.

On one occasion I had a vision. I saw myself walking along
the street, full of joy. In front of me walked an old man,
carrying two full buckets with difficulty. A voice inside me
said: "Take one of the buckets from that old man." I did so.
The bucket was very heavy. My joy grew less. Then the voice
said: "Take the other bucket, too." I took it. I was now
perspiring under my burden. My spiritual exaltation was at
an end, whereas the old man was now overjoyed.

In Bucharest there lived an Indian hypnotist, who was married to a half-Jewish lady. He had adopted a Jewish girl, his wife's daughter by her first marriage.

The girl had not been baptised. When the Fascist regime came to power, he asked us to baptise her, as he imagined this to be a mere formality. When he realised that we insisted on conversion before baptism, he gave up the idea. He no longer came to visit us, nor did the girl, although she felt attracted to Christ.

She went to see a Greek Orthodox priest, and asked him: "What shall I do to be saved?" (This was in the time of the Nazis, when the baptism of Jews was forbidden.) The priest answered: "As you are a Jewess, it is difficult. But send an application to the Patriarchy. It is possible that they will authorise it." The girl did not send in her application, but she poured water over her own head, saying: "In the name of the Father, and of the Son, and of the Holy Ghost, I baptise myself." With that she was easy in her mind.

The years went by. One Sunday morning, before going to church, I knelt down to ask God's blessing on the sermon I had prepared. As I did so, I heard a voice saying clearly: "The sermon you have prepared is not suitable for today. You must preach about Christianity and hypnosis." I argued with the voice, insisting that I was not prepared to talk on such an exacting subject. There was only a quarter of an hour to go before the service was due to start. And when all was said and done, to whom would I talk about this subject? I could think of no one in our church who was interested in it. But I obeyed the voice. On my way to church I hastily gathered together a few ideas.

After the service, a young lady approached me, whom I failed to recognise. It was the daughter of the hypnotist, now grown up. She asked me: "How did you know that I was going to come here today, and what made you prepare a sermon with a subject especially designed for me, who grew up in the aura of hypnosis?"

The girl had been ill for a week, and had promised God that if she recovered she would come to our church. I baptised her. She took her mother with her to our services and she, too, was converted and became a celebrated Christian poetess, publishing two collections of poems in honour of Jesus.

She became a valiant worker in God's vineyard. Unexpectedly one day she was given permission to preach the gospel in the women's prison in Bucharest. She also provided material assistance to the prisoners, who suffered terribly from lack of nourishment. She frequently visited the prison.

In the prison, which I often visited in her company, I had an interesting encounter.

Some years previously, walking through the streets one day with a Jewish brother, I had seen the sign of a fortune-teller, who boasted that she could tell anything about a person's past, present and future. Judging by her name, she might have been a Jewess.

Both of us went into her office. She asked us what we wanted. I told her that I, too, was a fortune-teller, and that I had come to see her, not as a client, but as a colleague. She was delighted, and told her maid to fetch us coffee. She used cards for telling fortunes. I told her that I used a book, the Bible. I read her a passage from Deuteronomy 18.10: "There shall not be found among you any one . . . that useth divination, or an observer of times, or an enchanter, or a witch." I interpreted the passage to her, and concluded: "Unless you are converted, you will perish. Now I have told your fortune, and it is a prophecy promised by God."

Two days later I read in the paper that the fortune-teller and her sister had been murdered by the maid, for her money. Years later, I met the maid again, in prison. She was converted, and became our sister.

Now let me recount some more examples of unusual spiritual phenomena.

A Mosaic Jewess, who was blind, married a Rumanian who was likewise blind. They had married without ever setting eyes on one another. But another woman came between them. The blind man left his wife, and set up house with her rival. The blind woman, poor and desperate, decided to take her own life. She gradually built up a small stock of sleeping tablets. One afternoon she dissolved them in a glass of water, but—as she later told us—just as she was about to drain the glass she clearly saw Jesus in the room. He said: "What you are doing is evil. I will show you a much better way." "Which way?" she asked. "Life has passed me by. I no longer have anything to hope for." Jesus answered: "Do as I say and you will be happy. Go to the other woman and tell her to come and stay with your husband in your house, and be her serving-maid. Serve them with all your love, without a spark of jealousy, and I shall make you happy!"

She followed this advice, and the other two moved in. She tended and cared for them in every possible way.

After her vision, she became interested in Jesus. She was converted, and I baptised her. (It is interesting to note that I baptised Jews, a thing that was forbidden by law at that time, in the house of a converted anti-Semite.) She obtained a Bible in braille, and found consolation in the Saviour, so that all grief vanished from her soul. Later, her husband quarrelled with the other woman, and life returned to normal.

All went well until a doctor, who was a member of our congregation, started treating her, in an attempt to restore her sight. As soon as she could see a little, she was attracted by the things of this world. She forgot her vision and the re-demption she had enjoyed.

A man who had held a high position under the Communist regime in Rumania, lost it when he was falsely informed against. In despair, he plunged a knife into his stomach, and collapsed in a pool of blood. One of our brethren, who lived opposite, was just sitting down to his dinner when an in-explicable impulse compelled him to leave the table and hurry to the man's flat. In a flash he saw what had happened, and called out: "Do you wish to fall into the hands of Satan?" As he helped the man, he told him of the Saviour. His life was saved. But who had told the brother to walk into the flat? This question, and the warning he had been given about Satan, started him thinking. Today he is our brother in the faith, and is witnessing for Jesus in Israel.

For us, such experiences as these were accepted as a part

of normal life for a Christian. Both my wife and my son have seen Jesus in our house. My son saw Him when he was about five or six years old. He chanced to tell us about it a long time afterwards. He was not amazed at seeing Jesus, and did not consider it necessary to mention it to anyone.

Just as a visitor from a distant place brings a gift to the one he loves, so I have tried to give my readers a faint impression of our encounters with the Invisible World, without necessarily placing these experiences on a high plane. God works in man in various ways and without his knowledge. He has spread His love over all creatures and all events, even the most ordinary, and in this way He can be seen in every lowly beggar and in every beautiful flower. We see God aright when we see Him everywhere. But I would certainly not claim that experience of these unusual phenomena is a necessity for the Christian life.

6

CONVERSATIONS WITH ZIONISTS AND OTHER JEWS

The sins of the Jews

DURING THE WAR, the International Red Cross had organised the immigration of Jews into Palestine. When the question arose of sending a group of Christian Jews, a Zionist leader vigorously opposed this move: "We do not want renegades. We shall throw them into the sea."

We encountered this kind of hostility in conversations with leading Zionists. We could understand their point of view, but we, too, had our national feelings.

In the Gospels Galilee is called Jesus's fatherland and Nazareth His town. Jesus did not consider Himself to be a citizen of the world, as did the Stoics, but a Jew, and He loved His people. There is a sort of nationalism which is an integral part of Christianity: the desire to work together for the greatest spiritual, economic, political and cultural benefit of one's own people. If you do not love your own people, how can you love foreigners?

The Christian Jews, each in his profession, have fulfilled their obligations to their people, and they do so in Israel too, playing their full part in developing and defending the country.

Christian Jews have served their people in a very special manner by opposing anti-Semitism, in a way of which other Jews were incapable.

During the Fascist regime, I was travelling by train from Galatz. The only other occupants of my compartment were Jewish businessmen. I talked to them about Jesus, but they were quite indifferent. At Ploesti, a burly Fascist entered the compartment. He seemed almost to smell that we were Jews. No sooner had he taken his seat than he began to be offensive, addressing us as "circumcised", "sidelocks", and by other similar names.

The others endured it in silence. I gave him time to calm down, and then I opened my Bible and showed him a number of passages which proved that Jesus was a Jew. I told him that the gospel mentions Jesus's circumcision. Christians believe that the Song of Solomon is a prophetic book about Jesus. In this book it is written: "My head is filled with dew, and my locks with the drops of the night" (Song of Sol. 5.2). So Jesus, too, must have had sidelocks. "If you make fun of Jews," I told him, "you are making fun of Jesus, too."

I went on: "I suppose that, like every Christian, you expect the return of Christ. The first time He came, He came as a Jew with sidelocks in Palestine. If He should choose to come a second time as a Jew with sidelocks to Rumania, you would mock Him and beat Him. What sort of a Christian are you?" He apologised, and admitted that up till then no one had ever spoken to him about these things.

In ways like these we also serve our people.

But we realised that we had another duty: it is not enough merely to show the anti-Semites their sins. The Jews, too, have their national failings, which must be made clear to them.

We could not agree with Dubnow or Grätz in their view of the history of the Jews. According to these writers, in all their conflicts with other nations, and at all times in history, the Jews have been in the right. We have always been innocent victims, and other people hate us without reason.

Historians often tend to write in precisely the same manner about other nations, and this is not right. I have no time for those who assert that the negroes, the whites, the Americans or the Russians are always right. Every social group has its sins. We Jews, too, have our sins, and Jewish sin has many aspects.

Economically, we exploit the countries in which we live, by appropriating a larger proportion of a country's wealth than is due to us in relation to our numbers. This is a general characteristic which does not mean that all Jews are exploiters. Many of them are terribly poor, some even live in slums. Most Jews lead an honest, productive life.

There is an explanation for our share in the national income. Jews live mainly in towns, and for this reason they enjoy the high standard of living that exists there. In the second place, they were excluded from the guilds of craftsmen in the Middle Ages, and as a result a great many Jews devoted themselves to business and banking. To this day they play an important role in the commercial and financial life of many countries, and often amass great wealth.

A Gentile exploiter, be he Rumanian, German or French, proceeds in exactly the same way as a Jew. "Anti-Semitism is the Socialism of the foolish," Engels once said, because it attacks only Jewish exploiters, and leaves the others alone. This is true, but there are a great many fools. When the exploiter belongs to a different race, the social problem becomes a national one.

Not all Jews are blameless for being hated. There is something else which arouses the animosity of other people. Compared with other races, Jews enjoy great intellectual superiority. As I have already mentioned, over sixty per cent of the Nobel prizewinners have been Jews, and nuclear science, the great scientific achievement of the twentieth century, is to a very great extent in Jewish hands. A Jew, Sternfeld, was the chairman of the Committee for Russian Astronautical Co-ordination. Jews hold key positions in political, economic and cultural life.

If all these were used for the purpose of establishing the Kingdom of God, a kingdom of justice, peace and joy on earth—which is the special task of the Jewish people—then the nightmare in which mankind lives today would come to an end. As the Apostle Paul said, if the world is reconciled to God by the rejection of the Jews, what will their acceptance be but life from the dead? (Rom. 11.15).

The other nations feel that there is a great deal the Jews could do for them, which they are not doing. A member of an anti-Semitic organisation was sentenced to twenty years' imprisonment. We met in a prison cell. He was in despair. He clasped my hand, and said: "Do something for the world, you Jews! Only you can do it."

What is the use of a knife that will not cut, a pen that will not write, a watch that will not show the time? What is the use of a Jewish race which does not conscientiously, systematically and thoroughly fulfil its role as the people chosen to bring light to nations and to turn their steps towards God?

Jesus said to the Jews: "Ye are the salt of the earth; but if the salt has lost its savour, wherewith shall it be salted? It is thenceforth good for nothing, but to be cast out, and to be trodden under foot of men" (Matt. 5.13). Anti-Semitism has given us more than enough of this tragic fate. Crimes have been committed against us which cannot be defended. But are we all entirely innocent? I would not assert it about myself.

Discussion in a prison cell

When, in solitary confinement, I heard from a new prisoner, by means of our system of tapping in code on the walls, about the creation of the new state of Israel, I was overjoyed. Afterwards, in a common cell, I spoke to an extreme right-winger of the Zionist movement. He had avoided me for a long time because, as he put it, we were both hard nuts, and he could see no point in our meeting. But an explanation was necessary, so God arranged for us to meet in a prison cell. He was a strong personality who made a great impression on his fellow men. Torture, and the deprivation of all creature comforts in his old age, never made him feel sorry for himself, but proved an opportunity for him to summon his strength and energy to continue the fight.

I had preached in the cell about the crucifixion of Jesus, and this was followed by a discussion, in which he openly expressed his opinion.

"Your continual dwelling on the sufferings of Jesus is a sign of masochism, and your constant glorification of the virgin birth merely stimulates the libido. A normal person doesn't continually think about a girl's virginity. It shows how your subconscious must be working. Christianity is a religion of neurotics. It can still satisfy the religious needs of some of its converts. But Judaism is the religion of life, normal life in all its fulness; it has nothing to do with a crucified Saviour. Our sins were expiated by the sacrifice of Isaac, which Abraham intended to make, but which was not carried out."

I asked him: "If Christianity is a false religion, and the Jewish people, as God's chosen people, are in the right, how can you explain the deep cleft between God and the Jewish people? Why are we punished by God and scattered among the nations?"

He replied: "We are not punished by God. The dispersion is our mission. The ghetto prepares us for the fulfilment of our ancient belief that the day will come when Israel will spread among all lands. In order that this ideal shall be fulfilled, we are scattered over the world; but we are not under any curse."

I pointed out that this is a contradiction of the Jewish prayer book, which repeatedly maintains: "For our sins' sake we are driven from our land." It also contradicts what is written in the Old Testament: "If thou wilt not hearken unto the voice of the Lord thy God . . . ye shall be plucked from off the land whither thou goest to possess it. And the Lord shall scatter thee among all peoples, from the one end of the earth even unto the other" (Deut. 28. 15, 63, 64).

He stuck to his point of view: "In the dispersion God is just as close to us as He was at the foot of Mount Sinai. The rabbis who wrote the prayer book admit their guilt because they are humble. And the curses that Moses pronounced are a blot on an otherwise great character."

"Did Moses pronounce these curses?" I asked. "He maintained that it was God."

He answered categorically: "They were only the words of Moses, and we are not guilty. We are Jehovah's favourite children, and we are fulfilling the mission He gave us. You have joined the ranks of the anti-Semites."

I thought it best to ignore this jibe, and went on: "Apparently what you are trying to say is that it is the mission of Israel to spread the Law of Moses, with which you yourself are only partly in agreement, and belief in the God of Israel. Quite certainly this mission still exists. But you must be half blind if you fail to see that it is only realised through Jesus. Where-ever in the world a Gentile prays to the God of Israel, and recognises the divine authority of the Jewish Bible, and the Jewish prophets as authorities, this is due to the Church that was founded by Jesus, and in no way to the merit of a Mosaic Jew. If the Mosaic Jews had committed no other sin—and in that case they would have surpassed the angels in heaven—they have at least committed the sin of not fulfilling their mission, but only talking about it and leaving it to others, thus increasing their guilt."

My opponent suddenly abandoned the theme of divine mission and contradicted what he had already said by declaring mockingly: "You will not be able to complain much longer about us. Our aim as Zionists is to go back to the land that was ours, a great deal of which is still wrongfully occupied by the Arabs. Then we shall leave you all in peace. Christian Jews will have to choose between being Jews and being Christians. If they choose the former, they must join us; if the latter, they must stay with their co-religionists."

"We want to come with you," I assured him, "though I admit that this will create difficulties, as we wish to come and yet to retain our Christian convictions."

"We do not want to interfere in your private affairs," he declared. "After all, you may believe, or not believe, whichever you wish."

"That is precisely where difficulties will arise," I said. "Our Christian faith will not remain bottled up inside us, nor will it be satisfied with the assurance of our own eternal salvation. It manifests its nature in true thinking, and in an impartiality which is certain to make things difficult for you. Take the Arab problem, which you mentioned. The Arabs have been in Palestine for centuries; it would be wrong to say that they have seized the country unlawfully. You might as well insist that the Americans should be driven out of the United States, so that the country could be returned to the Red Indians. If we went to Palestine, we should feel differently from some of you. The Arabs would be our brothers. We are opposed to chauvinism. The whole of Jerusalem and Israel belong rightfully to the Jews, but the utmost must be done that the Arabs should feel at home with us."

He shouted: "If you do that, you will be severely dealt with. The Christian countries have not behaved in a Christian way towards us, and we shall not allow anyone to start experimenting with Christian love towards our enemies in Palestine, of all places, where our national interests are at stake."

I could not allow him to condemn the whole of Christianity. "Many Christians have behaved in a Christian way towards the Jews. All the pietiests have done so, and the Scandinavian Lutherans and a great many Catholics, both laymen and clergy. So have some members of the Greek Orthodox Church. You are quick to notice the bad characteristics of Christians, but you close your eyes to the good ones. Where the spirit of their faith is missing, where their Christianity is a mere formality, it might go hand in hand with anti-Semitism. But beyond doubt there have been innumerable believing Christians who have loved you. In any case, your chauvinism is not at all representative of Jewish feelings. Most of our people would agree rather with a policy of love and understanding. Real Zionism is ethically Christian because, while fighting for the Jewish cause, it has feelings of friendship toward Arabs."

A well-known anti-Semite, who up till now had listened in silence, interrupted us: "Mr. Wurmbrand, you as both a Jew and a Christian would best be able to explain something to us Rumanians: is there or is there not a Jewish plot against the Gentiles, led by a clandestine Jewish government called Kahal?"

I replied, "There is no plot engineered by the Jews. Non-Jewish people, if they follow their true instincts, do both good and evil, without entering into any prior agreement. The Jews behave in the same way, without the existence of a Kahal. There are enormous differences among the Jews, between parties and denominations. Communist Jews imprison Zionist Jews, as you have an excellent opportunity of seeing. Nevertheless the Jews are united, not by a Kahal, but by their national characteristics, and this is true also of other nations. The special Jewish characteristics sometimes produce positive results of enormous value, sometimes negative results, like their attitude to Christ. This attitude we consider to be a real curse to the nations of the world, who are aware of it without understanding it, because it postpones the only possible solution of the world crisis, which is the establishment of the Kingdom of God, based on justice and happiness, of which only Christ can be the head. This curse must be changed into a blessing, by converting the Jews to a belief in Jesus, because they are called to be God's main tool in establishing His kingdom. Anti-Semitism, too, is a curse, because it prevents the conversion of the Jews."

The anti-Semite answered: "You will never wipe out hostility towards the Jews. They are incapable of being assimilated; they remain an alien element in every country. Every organism has a natural tendency to eliminate foreign bodies."

I admitted: "The Jews are quite different from other people. Their unique history proves this. They cannot be assimilated. But in His parable of the Good Samaritan, Jesus taught us, not that we should absorb people from other nations, but that we should behave justly and kindly to them, whoever they are. There is no justification for anti-Semitism."

The anti-Semite, who refused to let me resume my conversation with the Zionist, maintained his conviction: "A nation must defend itself. Not only are the Jews incapable of being assimilated, but they would like to assimilate us to their own mentality. They undermine our national institutions."

I replied: "So far as that is concerned, you have already been defeated: you are all living in a state of perfect Judaism. If you want to get rid of Judaic influence, you must renounce Christianity, capitalism and Communism; you must give up Singer sewing machines, Waxmann's streptomycin, much of the realm of microphysics, Einstein's theory of the universe, everything that sets is seal on twentieth-century man, and return to the primitive state of a pastoral tribe. After all, it is a fact that man rules nature, and that the white races are at present the most advanced. It is also a fact that, for better or worse, the Jewish mentality is the dominant one. The Jews have an unsurpassed knack of imposing their ideas on others, and in this respect they are invincible, though this is not necessarily always to their credit. But neither is it always to their discredit. People like you are trying to get rid of the Jews while at the same time you worship Jesus, who was Himself born a member of our race."

I turned to the Zionist and added: "We Christian Jews, too, have this quality of invincibility. What is more, we are the most perfect incarnation of the belief in humanitarianism, which contains the core of Judaism. We are the true bearers of Judaic values."

He answered: "You are heretics of the Jewish faith. As a Protestant, you are also a heretic of the Christian faith. Double heretic! We may be friends, but it is impossible to reconcile our principles. Your words really conceal a seething hatred of everything that is dear to us, just as the Red Flag is a cover for hatred. Marx wrote an anti-Semitic book, *The Jewish Question*. The Communist International, too, has published its thesis on the Jewish problem in a book by Heller called *The End of Judaism*. We are hated everywhere, utterly hated."

Mere words are powerless to help people who have suffered greatly, and have reached the stage when they see enmity in people who are not their enemies.

For this reason I decided to change the subject, so I said: "In a book which you published in 1934, you wrote that Jewish immigration to the part of Palestine which was placed at your disposal would reach a critical point when Palestine cannot absorb any more Jews. An overwhelming majority of Jews will have to remain scattered among the other nations, and you must stop imagining that you are surrounded only by enemies. A new adjustment will be necessary, but your anti-Christian attitude would make this adjustment difficult.

Besides, the falling away from the Mosaic religion goes on more rapidly in Palestine than in the dispersion. Only a small percentage of Jews in Palestine go to the synagogues or keep the Jewish traditions. What do you say to this?"

He answered: "We are back in our own land. At last we shall be able to strip off the expensive and deadly garments of the Chosen Race. We shall be just like any other nation."

"You are contradicting yourself," I reminded him. "A few minutes ago you were talking about the holy mission of Israel, Jehovah's favourite child."

He laughed. "Now we are in Palestine we shall complete our mission, by sending apostles to foreign nations. But on a material plane we shall live like them. We shall have our own army, and it will give us victory. We shall have tractors, and they will be our Messiah."

I pointed out: "And one day we shall die, leaving behind us our torturers and our victims, because in the countries where we have lived we have not only been killed, but we have also killed. Consider the millions who were killed by Trotsky, Bela Kun, Tibor Szamuely, Rakosi, Ana Pauker, Jews who were rulers in Communist countries. We shall also leave behind our tractors, and we shall stand before the judgement of God. We shall have to answer for all we have done, and even more for what we have left undone, because we have not been obedient bearers of light. Judaism has shone like a beacon. Salvation has come, and still comes, from the Jews, as Jesus said. But it comes only from the Judaism that was incarnate in Jesus. The spirit that unites all nations does not come from the Jews, who refused to allow other nations to enter the temple, but from Jesus. The sense of supreme justice does not come from the Jews, whose ultimate revelation is the Old Testament (a very valuable book, but one which contains commands to utterly destroy innocent people). It comes from Jesus. Jesus was the first to preach a just and impartial God, who reveals Himself through love to every nation that seeks Him."

The Zionist was content to answer: "We are prepared to make a gift of Christianity to the nations, and we shall see how they make it come true. Let them endure being struck on the face, and let them turn the other cheek! We have put up with blows all too long. We no longer want the religion of meekness."

In prison, serious discussions cannot last long. The anti-Semite seized this moment to make a joke: "We shall receive Christianity as a present from you, minus the commandment about committing adultery. Jewesses are very beautiful. We are against the Jews, but not against Jewesses!"

In the unclean atmosphere produced by a joke of this kind the Spirit no longer vibrates. I held my peace. What our feeble words are incapable of doing, God can do. He will fulfil his plans of peace, even that of peace between Jews and Arabs. He has made the miracle of giving the Jews the victory in the Six-Day War. We hope for an even bigger miracle, lasting peace between Israel and Arabs, with a Jewish Jerusalem serving as lighthouse for the Moslem world. Jews and Arabs can become friends at the foot of the cross of Jesus.

"*I shall stick to our old religion*"

I spoke to another Zionist leader, and asked him: "I realise that you are compelled to attack us. But why do you do it in such a vulgar manner?"

He answered: "We choose our method according to public taste. An academic style would not be very convincing."

"Let us forget it," I replied. "In Paul's Epistle to the Romans, the Christian Church is compared to a branch grafted on to the olive tree of Jewry. Do you realise what this means? An organisation embracing more than a thousand million people, and which plays an enormous role in history, is described in the sacred book of this religion as the lawful property of the Jews. Surely we are not so strong, wealthy and self-confident that we can forego a position of this kind? In the sacred book of a thousand million people Jesus is referred to as the Glory of Israel (Luke 2.32). Can we who are so despised afford to renounce this glory?"

He retorted: "We decline it; we refuse to have anything to do with Jesus and Christianity."

I asked him: "In whose name do you decline? Whom do

you represent? Does the intellectual élite speak on behalf of the nation? Because almost without exception the intellectual élite of the Jewish people in the twentieth century have supported Jesus."

I quoted from *As I See the World* by Albert Einstein, where he said that if we cleanse the Judaism of the prophets, and Christianity, as Jesus preached it, from all its later additions, especially from priestcraft, we shall have a doctine which will be able to heal mankind of all its social ills. It is the duty of all good people, he said, to strive earnestly to introduce into their milieu this really humane teaching, as far as lies in their power.

I continued: "The synagogue refused to bury Henry Bergson, because he had openly avowed that he was a disciple of Jesus. Franz Werfel, the great Jewish poet, wrote in praise of St. Bernadette. Scholem Asch, the great Jewish novelist, was a Christian. Nils Bohr and Piccard are Christian Jews, and there are many like them. Emil Ludwig wrote *The Son of Man*, a book full of admiration for his subject. This is also true of Max Brod. Not to mention Martin Buber, who called Jesus his elder brother.

"These, after all, are representative leaders of the Jewish race. This is the first time in history that the intellectual leaders of Judaism have rallied to Jesus. In this way, a biblical prophecy is being fulfilled, just as the return of the Jews to Palestine, and the fact that Jews fill leading positions in so many countries, fulfil other biblical prophecies."

The Zionist leader laughed: "All the people you mention were converted to Christianity in their old age, when people tend to suffer from a hardening of the arteries. I don't bother my head with religion, but if we must have one, I shall stick to our old religion."

It was impossible to get him to see reason. He did not know that the old religion familiar to Abraham was salvation by faith, which the Christians preach; and that the new religion is really the Mosaic religion, where salvation is the fruit of obedience to commandments that were not written down until four hundred years after the death of Abraham.

Another factor that distinguished us from the Zionists was

that for them the national question was of supreme importance. We were certainly not blind to it, but for us it was of minor significance.

We are at one with the Zionists in one thing. We are in favour of Israel. The rights of the Jews to Palestine are unchallengeable. God, the creator of the universe, gave them this country.

As for the Arabs, it is simply nonsense for them to be afraid of the Jews. What can three million Jews do to three hundred million Arabs? The Arabs should rather profit and learn from the intellectual and financial superiority of their new neighbours. I should also expect the Vatican and the World Council of Churches to take a clear stand on the side of Israel.

We made our position clear.

The Jews enjoy intellectual and material advantages which the Arabs do not possess. The Jews must show understanding, kindness, indulgence, and a willingness to help the Arab world. Difficulties can be overcome by showing them love.

How effective it would be to bombard the impoverished Egyptians with bread, medicine and words of peace! Christian nations could proceed in the same manner. Attacked, the Jewish people must defend themselves with military weapons. But the basic attitude of the heart must be love. The Arabs are loved by every true Jew. They deserve love as much as every other human being.

All things to all men

The doctrine which the Zionists found it particularly hard to swallow was the commandment that men should love their enemies.

Would any Zionist have done what we did? After Rumania had severed its alliance with Nazi Germany, it was decreed that any person concealing members of the German army would be liable to the death penalty, as all Germans were to be handed over as prisoners of war. A number of girls serving in the German army, the so-called *Blitzmädchen*, appealed to us to shelter them, to save them from being deported to Russia. Naturally, we did so.

Some person or other informed on us, and the police surrounded the house. A police commissar entered, and asked me: "Are you sheltering German girls?" I answered: "Do you know what my nationality is?" He said: "Richard Wurmbrand? You're German, of course." I showed him my identity card, issued during the Fascist regime, which stated that I was of Jewish race. "I am a Jew," I declared. "Half of my family have been murdered by the Nazis. Do you really imagine that I would shelter German girls?"

The officer apologised: "The whole thing is obviously a mistake," he admitted, and withdrew. The girls were in an adjoining room. We made no distinction, as God makes no distinction either, allowing the sun to shine and the rain to fall on good and evil alike.

On other occasions we intervened successfully on behalf of Germans who were threatened with deportation only because they were Germans. It was a crime similar to persecuting men only because they were Jews.

In time, this activity became widely known. The Zionists could not forgive us for it, any more than they had forgiven Jesus for giving His love to Romans and Samaritans alike, even to publicans, who were traitors to their country. It was even insinuated that He was on their side, because people failed to realise that the love which He bestowed on sinners did not mean that He condoned their transgressions, but that this would heal their minds. Neither did we condone Nazism, but we healed some of the Nazis by deeds of love.

Our position as Christian Jews is always between the devil and the deep blue sea; as we tried to win everyone to the faith, to be all things to all men, we were almost like actors striving in different plays to interpret completely different characters.

By way of putting me to shame, someone once described me as a great actor. I took this as a compliment. I cannot see how it is possible to be a good missionary unless one has a certain artistic flair, and a knack of playing different roles.

One day I left my house to carry out my duty as a fisher of men. The first person I talked to was a noted anti-Semite.

"I don't want to hear about Jesus, because he was a dirty Jew," he rebuffed me. I replied: "How do you know Jesus was a dirty Jew? He is the Son of God, and belongs to no one nation. In driving the merchants from the temple He showed his repugnance for a quality which you condemn in Jews, the pursuit of money. The harshest words of condemnation ever written about Jews are to be found in the New Testament. Your place is at the side of Jesus, not with those who condemned Him to death."

I parted from him, and met a Jew, who told me that he did not believe in Jesus, because He was the Saviour only of the Gentiles. I asked him: "Where did you get that from? Jesus was a Jew. The New Testament opens with the words: 'Jesus Christ, the son of David, the son of Abraham', giving His entire genealogy and proving that He is of Jewish descent. In the Scriptures Jesus is called 'the Glory of His people Israel'. He loved His people passionately, and told a Samaritan woman: 'Salvation comes from the Jews' (John 4.22). Christianity is essentially a vast undertaking to Judaise the world, because it has been ordained that people of all races shall become 'Jews in their hearts'. Even after Jesus had been crucified, the apostles continued to call Jerusalem the Holy City, and the apostle Paul writes that the Jews are still loved by God for the sake of their forefathers, and that they will play a great role in the future. The chosen ones of heaven will consist of 144,000 people from the twelve tribes of Israel alone."

Shortly afterwards, I ran into a brother who was full of confidence in his own faith, but not conspicuous for his good deeds. As I was familiar with his way of life, I said to him: "Faith without good deeds is dead" (Jas. 2.17), because men will be judged by what they do.

I then visited a believer who was on the brink of despair because of a sin he had committed. He could never forgive himself, and he doubted whether he was saved. I explained that man is regarded as true to his faith, even without good deeds, because God looks on the heart, and not on our actions; the opposite, in fact, of what I had just said to the last man I had met.

After these four conversations I sat down on a park bench.

My head was spinning. I asked myself which of the four things I had said I believed myself. The answer I came to was that the different ways in which one speaks to people are nothing but bait with which to lure them to Him who is far above and beyond our prejudices and ideas. But going from one category of human being to another involves the use of different arguments and different medicines for the soul. The anti-Semite and the Jew brought to conversion will meet in the same Christian love, but work of this kind is very exhausting.

Anti-Klausner

A professor at the university in Jerusalem, Josef Klausner, wrote a book called *Jesus of Nazareth*, which has been translated into all the main world languages.

Every time I talked to a Jew about the Saviour, he would conclude his argument with: "The problem of Jesus has been explained by Klausner." Generally the learned Jew concerned had not taken the trouble to read Klausner, but he had the book unopened on his bookshelves, and this was enough. He did not need to bother his head any more with Jesus.

For this reason I considered it necessary to publish an answer to Klausner's book, which I called *The Jews and Jesus of Nazareth. Anti-Klausner*.

Klausner took an unfair advantage of his great name, which made him confident that his assertions would be accepted by the rank and file of Jews, and enabled him to make statements which were completely untrue but which would never be subject to any check.

He writes, for example, that in Paul we find no authentic historical proof of Jesus's life and work.

Any student familiar with the Scriptures could have corrected the professor on this point.

In Paul we find a great many details about the life of Jesus. He says, for example, that Jesus was betrayed, that He was killed by the Jews, and that the place of His crucifixion was just outside Jerusalem. Paul also tells us something about the mind of Jesus. He says that Christ "loved the church and gave himself for it" (Eph. 5.25). He describes Jesus's humility, His

mildness and His power. Above all, he constantly reminds us
of a "biographical detail" that Klausner has omitted, namely
that Jesus rose from the dead.

Without any historical basis in fact, Klausner proceeds to
make any statement that suits him. He says that Jesus was
born in Nazareth. Where did he get this? Any mention of
Bethlehem, which the Gospels describe as Jesus's birthplace,
would be rather awkward, because it is David's town, and it
was here that the prophets foretold that the Messiah would be
born.

He claims the story of Salome is a legend. Professor Klausner
merely decides that this is so, and argument is superfluous.

"John the Baptist considered himself to be Elias." The
Gospels state that when John was asked: "Are you Elias?",
he answered: "I am not." (John 1.21). Professor Klausner
possesses a source of information which is not available to
other people.

He goes on to say that it is obvious that John the Baptist
knew nothing of Jesus, and did not accept Him as the Messiah.
The only historical sources, the Gospels, state that Jesus and
John were related, and that the latter proclaimed Jesus as the
Messiah. No one knows where Klausner obtained his in-
formation.

The only argument Klausner uses every time he submits a
statement for which there is no proof is: "It is obvious that
this is so."

He excuses Judas Iscariot, proclaiming him to be a learned
Jew with a clear understanding. The account of Jesus being
betrayed by a trick is only a legend.

Just as all the unsavoury details about Judas are dismissed, so
all the lovable features attributed to Jesus are also put down as
legend. Klausner refuses to believe that Jesus on the Cross
would have said of His executioners: "Father, forgive them; for
they know not what they do" (Luke 23.34). His argument is
simply that Jesus could not have pronounced these words
in such terrible circumstances. I have personally known men
and women, disciples of Jesus, who have spoken the same words
under cruel torture, and what is more, who took the first oppor-

tunity of doing good to those who had tortured them. But Professor Klausner has simply made up his mind that love of this kind is non-existent.

He swiftly dismisses the gospel story of the resurrection of of Jesus by declaring that it is obvious (a wonderful expression which relieves the author of the need to adduce any proof) that Joseph of Arimathea removed the body from the tomb.

He believes "a resurrection is incomprehensible." There are a great many things that are incomprehensible. Incomprehensible though it may appear, there actually exists a learned professor who, instead of starting off by analysing facts and documents, proceeds on the basis of certain prejudices as to what God can or cannot do.

After writing hundreds of pages without making any contribution to the problem of the life of Jesus, Klausner discusses the differences between Judaism and the teaching of Jesus. In this connection he states that a nation cannot survive by means of an abstract faith and by a universal human ethic. It needs a practical form of religion, involving forms capable of expressing religious ideas, and capable of penetrating everyday life with the sanctity of religion. "Jesus has not shown us new ways for our national life." By accepting the teaching of Jesus, "national life and the national state would entirely disappear." "His doctrine contains no elements which can maintain the state and regulate the community." "Jesus came to abolish culture."

What answer is one to give to this two thousand years after the coming of Jesus? Professor Klausner has obviously never heard of Christian culture, he knows nothing of the national states which still exist, which were established and maintained thanks to Christianity. How can he explain the fact that all the nations of Europe and America, as well as a great many African nations, have independent national states, despite the fact that they have accepted Christianity, which, according to Klausner, destroys state, nation and culture?

I might go on to ask: "What did the enemies of Jesus, Caiaphas, Annas and the others, do to the Jewish state?" They succeeded in removing the great danger that Jesus represented, on the pretext that this was necessary if the Jewish national state was to be maintained. These were the very men who led the Jewish state to disaster. History has proved that Christianity establishes and maintains a state, while Pharisaism destroys it. How can one possibly ignore these obvious historical proofs?

Klausner says that Judaism cannot accept the term "The Son of God", or only "God", for the Messiah, even though the idea in itself is Jewish. But if the idea of the Son of God is Jewish, then it is obvious that only those who have renounced the inheritance of their people can refuse to accept it. According to Klausner, who defies any form of logic, it is the renegades who have accepted the Jewish idea.

Klausner dislikes Jesus's teaching that we should love those who wrong us. Human society, he says, would not survive if every injury remained unpunished. But why did the Jewish national state disappear two thousand years ago? The Jews rose in revolt against the injustice of the Roman Empire. The result was that the Jewish state vanished from off the face of the earth. One might have expected the professor to conclude from this event, and thousands like it, that human society cannot survive if we repay evil with evil, if we rise against injustice. For thousands of years states have vanished, bloodthirsty wars have been fought, and thousands of millions of people have been killed because one side has refused to tolerate the injustices of the other, and has failed to requite evil with love. This is a historical fact. There are grave issues when violence is justified, but the fundamental attitude should be love.

When Jesus teaches love toward enemies, he does not mean literal practice of non-violence whatever happens around us. He Himself used violence of language and also the whip. The world is not yet conveniently arranged for non-violence. Sadly, you have sometimes to exterminate enemies of your nation. But nothing compels me to hate them. God does not look at our deeds dictated by circumstances. Here the desire to kill must be removed. Here only love must reign. In the end it will triumph also over external circumstances.

It is not wrong for a nation to practise love toward those who wrong it. Professor Klausner's reproach against Jesus is unjust. Nations do not as a rule vanish from off the face of the earth because they have practised love.

Klausner sums up his attitude neatly when he declares that Judaism is in its entirety of this world. It was for this reason that the Jews rejected Him whose kingdom is not of this world, but belongs to the sphere of purest truth. "He cannot be the Messiah of the Jewish people."

Now, if you want to decide whether a person is the Messiah or not, it would be scientifically correct if you first clearly defined what this term means, what methods exist for recognising the true Messiah, and, finally, investigate whether that person fulfils these conditions. Klausner did not carry out any studies of this nature. In my book I did it for him, pointing out that all the prophecies about the Messiah who expiates the sins of mankind by His suffering, and other biblical prophecies, were fulfilled by Jesus.

There are a great many of these prophecies, and a large body of literature exists about them. Without going into these in detail, it might be worth mentioning one, which is incapable of more than one interpretation, since it is based on mathematics.

The prophet Daniel, who lived about six hundred years B.C., foretold with astonishing accuracy the year in which the Messiah would be killed. This was the year when Jesus was crucified.

Anyone studying this prophecy with an open mind will realise that waiting for any other saviour is fruitless. The Talmud declares: "The time determined for the coming of the Messiah has passed, but the Messiah has not come." The Talmud, refusing Jesus as the Messiah had no other solution than to declare God to be a liar, because He did not keep His promise, and allowed the time foretold for the coming of the Messiah to go by without keeping His word.

Let us consider the biblical text: "Seventy weeks [of years] are determined upon thy people," the Archangel Gabriel declared to Daniel in about 600 B.C., "and upon thy holy city to finish the transgression, and to make an end of sins, and to make reconciliation for iniquity, and to bring in everlasting righteousness, and to seal up the vision and prophecy, and to anoint the most Holy. Know therefore and understand, that from the going forth of the commandment to restore and to build Jerusalem unto the Messiah the Prince, shall be seven weeks [of years], and threescore and two weeks [of years]; the street shall be built again, and the wall, even in troublous times. And after threescore and two weeks shall the Messiah be cut off, but not for himself . . ." (Dan. 9.24–26).

This would give us a total of sixty-nine weeks of years, in other words sixty-nine multiplied by seven, which is four hundred and eighty-three years, from the time when the order was given to rebuild Jerusalem to the death of the Messiah.

Let us check the events that actually occurred:

King Xerxes of Persia commenced his reign in the year 465 B.C. In the book of Nehemiah, Chapter 2, we read that in the twentieth year of his reign he permitted the rebuilding of Jerusalem. In other words, nineteen years had elapsed, which we must subtract. Consequently the order to rebuild Jerusalem was issued in the year 446 B.C.

Four hundred and eighty-three years after this event, the Messiah, according to the prophecy, would be killed. For the sake of accuracy, we should remember that Daniel calculated the year according to the old Jewish calendar, which consisted of three hundred and sixty days, unlike our calendar year which has three hundred and sixty-five and a quarter days.

This means that we must convert the Jewish calendar year to years based on our present reckoning:

483 years × 360 days (based on the Hebrew calendar) = 173,880 days.

173,880 days : 365¼ (the length of our present calendar year) = 476 years.

This means that four hundred and seventy-six years would elapse from the year 446 B.C. to the death of the Messiah. In other words, this event would occur in the year A.D. 30 calculated according to our calendar.

And it was precisely in this year that Jesus was crucified.

It is a well-established fact that in the sixth century A.D., when the pre-Christian and post-Christian eras were divided, there was a mathematical mistake in the calculation. The birth of Christ was assigned to a date four years later than it actually occurred. The year A.D. 30, by our modern calculations, is in fact the thirty-fourth year of Jesus's life. And in the thirty-fourth year of His life, in the year 30 of the Christian era, Jesus was crucified, precisely as prophesied by Daniel.

God's vengeance was not slow to strike. Daniel had foretold that after this unparalleled misdeed, "for the overspreading of abominations he shall make it desolate, even until the consummation, and that determined shall be poured upon the desolate." (Dan. 9.27) We know that, shortly afterwards, Palestine was ravaged by the army of Titus, that the land was utterly laid waste, the temple was burned, and sacrifices were no longer made.

Rashi, one of the leading biblical commentators, recognises that Titus fulfilled these very prophecies. But in this case the Messiah must be a man who was killed before Titus enjoyed his great triumph. This man is Jesus; it cannot be anyone else.

Professor Klausner was one of the many intellectual leaders of the Jews who was misled. It is astonishing that a race which is so intelligent and so civilised can accept a book which sets such low standards. In the last chapter of his book, Klausner plumbs the depths of the ridiculous with the remark that "Jesus became a Christian". This is written by a university professor. He might as well have said that Mohammed became a Mohammedan.

Is Jesus God?

There are a great many Jews who are prepared to accept the Christian moral code, but refuse to accept the Christian teaching about the divinity of Jesus.

I was one day in the office of an intellectual who was in this position. I asked him: "Are you really able to make the Christian moral code a reality in your life? You say you accept this code, and in fact you have called it 'glorious'."

He began to laugh. It is depressing how seldom one manages to start a really serious discussion with anyone. He said: "Yes, but one cannot demand that it should be put into practice."

I answered: "In my opinion it is just as ridiculous to give

mankind a moral code incapable of being carried out as it would be for a shoe manufacturer to make beautiful shoes that cannot be worn. The Christian moral code may appear incapable of being put into practice, but it is not so for everyone. The conditions necessary for keeping it must be fulfilled. Every businessman knows that income must cover expenditure. Christian morals involve certain expenses—loving, serving, helping. But where do you get the strength for this? From your faith, a treasure-house full of truths revealed by God."

"No, no," was his answer. "The Christian dogmas are absurd. How could I believe that a Jewish carpenter, who bought wood, boiled glue, sold his products and went about the everyday business of an ordinary man, could be God? The only form of Christianity the Jews could ever hope to approach would be Unitarianism. Jesus may be a great teacher, a great prophet, but never God."

I explained: "That possibility does not exist. Jesus assumed divine rights, and accepted worship that belongs only to God. If He is not God, He cannot have been a great teacher, but He must have been merely a fraud or a crazy fanatic. You would not dare to regard Him as such. The only alternative left, then, is to accept Him as God."

"We are in the sphere of words," he interrupted. "In ancient times a great many people were regarded as gods, and so were celestial bodies. Hercules, Romulus, and the emperors Julius and Augustus were regarded as gods. Even the mad Caligula was raised to the status of a divinity. The philosopher Epicurus was considered to be a god. Even among the early Christian fathers there were some who insisted that Christians become gods. In human speech, the word god is not a name reserved only for the Creator. In this sense we might perhaps call Jesus divine, just as we could call Plato divine, or talk about Beethoven's divine music. But no more!"

The position of a Protestant, when he is debating with a Jew, is much easier than that of a Greek Orthodox or a Roman Catholic. Protestants delight in their freedom of thought, and need never be afraid of making a statement in an incautious moment which Catholics would consider heretical.

My reply was: "As soon as we describe something or some-one as divine, we are moving in a sphere where words have lost their power. In what way is Jesus divine? And in what way is the Heavenly Father divine? The French are right when they say: '*Un Dieu défini est un Dieu fini*' (A God defined is a God who is finished). Lao-Tse said: 'Any *Dao* [god] who is named is not the true *Dao*.' In calling Jesus God, I mean that He cannot be compared with other human beings. His character is a miracle: He cannot be explained in terms of genetic laws, laws of environment and so on. In Him we have a fortunate combination of all the four human types: sanguine, choleric, phlegmatic and melancholic. The life of Jesus can only be explained by assuming that He comes from a higher sphere than the human.

"Brought up in a carpenter's workshop, without access to the wisdom of other nations and races, He gave the world, at the age of thirty, an unparalleled moral code. His death, side by side with two criminals, was followed by a miraculous spread of His religion. The best explanation of these facts is that Jesus is divine.

"We cannot judge on the basis of sympathy or antipathy, but only on the basis of proof. Let your understanding act like an impartial tribunal, which pronounces its verdict on the basis of proofs which are submitted to it. There are five highly convincing arguments in favour of the divine nature of Jesus.

"First, He overcame death, which no other human being has done.

"Second, He overcame physical laws which man cannot overcome (raising the dead, healing lepers, multiplying loaves and fishes, and so on).

"Third, He overcame Judaism, which wanted Him to remain unknown. False Messiahs, who were accepted by the Jews, such as Bar-kochba and Sabetai Zvi, are unknown to the rest of the world, whereas Jesus, who was rejected by us, is wor-shipped by hundreds of millions of people.

"Fourth, He conquered the Roman Empire. The great persecutor of Christianity, Julian the Apostate, died with these words on his lips: 'Thou has conquered, O Galilean.' It is the strongest who conquers: If Jesus has conquered kings, He is King of Kings.

"Fifth, by the madness of the Cross, He has overcome human wisdom. One after another, philosophical systems are destroyed. Who even remembers the anti-Christian philosopher Celsus, or of the Cult of Reason introduced by the French Revolution? Who still leads his life according to the Talmud? But the words of the carpenter, who is both man and God— 'Heaven and earth shall pass away, but my words shall not pass away' (Matt. 24.35)—are still valid. From the purely human point of view there was no chance whatever that Jesus's words would be fulfilled, nor was there any chance that His prophecy that His gospel would be spread to the ends of the earth would ever come true.

"In no possible way could Jesus be merely a human being, and for that reason we accept that He is God in human guise.

"It is important to know this. The medical advice given by a doctor's assistant carries very little real weight, and is not decisive. But the advice given by a well-known doctor comes into an entirely different category. You can lead a Christian life when you know that these laws come not from another person, who is fallible like yourself, but from God. It is this that makes it possible for people to keep God's commandments."

The intellectual Jew had no answer to make. He grew thoughtful. I was tired of having the last word; it is wiser to leave it to your opponent. It is difficult to win over to belief someone you have beaten in a debate, because in so doing you will have wounded his pride. In this case, I had the last word, and I did not win him.

7

OUR ATTITUDE TO COMMUNISM

Communism as part of God's plan

THE CHANGE IN the political regime in Rumania presented new problems for us.

Marxism had been practically unknown among us. Now, all young people were being educated in its spirit, and a great many Marxist and atheist books were being published.

The Jews played an important role in spreading the Communist ideology in our country. We ran up against it at every step, and were forced to adopt a new approach.

We published a series of pamphlets dealing with the problems of the relationship between Protestant Christianity and Marxism: *Conversation between a young Socialist and a Believer*, *Jesus and Socialism* (an answer to the book by the Socialist theorist Karl Kautsky, *The Origins of Christianity*), *Dialectic Materialism and Biblical Faith* (an answer to Engels' book *Anti-Dühring*) and *Karl Marx and Belief*. We tried to make these booklets attractive to Communist readers. On the first page of *Karl Marx and Belief* there was a picture of Marx, and on the next page a picture of "Jesus the Working Proletarian", followed by other pictures, such as "Jesus driving the Capitalists out of the Temple". There followed an account of Jesus's sacrifice.

We were in no way frightened by the atheist offensive, which persuaded a number of other people that Christianity was finished in our country. Christianity has many times in the past been declared dead. In *The History of the Popes*, Ranke describes the spread of heresy in Italy during the fifteenth and sixteenth centuries; at that time, too, it was believed that Christianity was at the end of its tether.

Nor were we terrified at the thought that a small group of real Christians were so feeble compared to the giant Goliath of atheism.

For myself, I clung to the biblical idea that the power of God is fulfilled only in weakness. The *Tao-Te-King*, the sacred book of Taoism, rightly declares: "All creatures and plants are delicate and weak when they are born, but when they perish, they are strong and powerful. What is strong and powerful is destroyed, and what is weak and delicate begins to live. For this reason a strong army does not conquer, but is destroyed like a strong tree. That which is strong and powerful does not have the same advantage as that which is weak and delicate."

It was precisely our weakness which gave us immense strength in our struggle with the all-powerful Marxism, which many Jews also championed.

If Communism exists in God's world, it must surely be to fill a vacuum in God's economy. Capitalism makes a man an individualist. Emphasis on personal salvation and personal sanctification reflects man's conscience in the social conditions created by capitalism. The very instigation of the Socialist set-up made a profound difference to the thinking of a great many Christians. They were able to stand face to face with Communists simply by showing that everything that is beautiful and attractive in Communism has been derived from Christianity.

Today the churches are divided. The Church of the early Christian Jews in Jerusalem, organised according to the instructions of Jesus himself to His apostles, was a Church in which all shared their possessions. In the Acts of the Apostles we read of the first Christians: "And the multitude of them that believed were of one heart and of one soul: neither said any of them that ought of the things which he possessed was his own; but they had all things common . . . Neither was there any among them that lacked: for as many as were possessors of lands or houses sold them, and brought the prices of the things that were sold, and laid them down at the apostles' feet: and distribution was made unto every man according as he had need" (Acts 4.32–35).

This was another kind of Communism, one based on love! It would be better not to use the same name for it, so different is it from what we experience under Communism today.

We could come to an understanding with many Communists, we could accept some of them as brothers, because not only did we preach the individual salvation of the soul through the blood of Jesus—which remained our main task—but we were also interested in social problems.

We believe that it is the duty of Christians to strive to ensure that men and women need not depart from the Christian standard; they should not be compelled to crawl, flatter, steal, kill in wars, or exploit other people, in order to enjoy material sufficiency.

We do not consider that sanctification is merely a personal matter; it is also a social vocation. Not only must I be glorified, but the social body must be glorified, by creating the kingdom of God on earth; in other words, a kingdom where justice, peace and joy reign. We must fight for just laws and institutions, as the first Christians created an ideal social institution, the Church, which has this characteristic too. We long for a social justice which springs from love, and is inspired by the wish to imitate God, who makes the sun to shine and the rain to fall on all alike.

We do not believe in all the saints canonised by the Orthodox and Roman Catholic Churches. Their legendary and unique deeds are enough to make us, ordinary people, despair. When Peter tried to walk on the water by himself, he sank. We want to walk in common with others along the road that leads to Jesus.

Jesus reproached whole towns for not being converted (Matt. 11.21–23); in other words, He expects conversion to be a social phenomenon, embracing large numbers of people.

In the parable of the Prodigal Son, the father is made to say: "Let us eat and be merry." There are no pleasures without food. We must make sure that everybody has food.

We must strive to convert not only a prostitute or a drunkard, but prostitution, alcoholism, the prisons, man's exploitation of other people, war—all these things must be abolished, and this can only be done if the Christian fights his battles in the social as well as the personal sphere. Evil has made great strides; there is a long line stretching from Cain, who killed a man with a staff, to the gas chambers of Auschwitz and the Communist extermination camps. The satanic powers have transferred their attack from the individual to an offensive on a large social front. The powers of good must do the same.

In the old days Paul could preach from the same pulpit as his enemies. We have a pulpit today, but our enemies have the schools, the press, large publishing concerns, the cinema, the radio, television. We, too, have a right to all these things, and if we are to achieve them, then we must strive to realise Daniel's prophecy that "the kingdom and dominion, and the greatness of the kingdom under the whole heaven, shall be given to the people of the saints of the most High" (Dan. 7.27).

The apostle Jude writes of the common salvation; and something like this does exist, not only personal salvation. Jacob prophesied of Jesus that "nations will gather around Him" (Gen. 49.10, according to the Hebrew). The nations, not an occasional individual here and there.

The conditions necessary for the establishment of God's kingdom on earth are now present; this was not possible when material conditions were so wretched. The advances of modern technology have made it possible for all people to have food and clothing. Modern medicine, freed from the shackles which still hamper it, could give us physically healthy men and women. Proper education and psychology could help us to give us people who are mentally healthy. Modern means of communication could ensure that a handful of people, filled with the spirit of God, could exercise a decisive influence for the benefit of all mankind. Modern scientific ways of thinking could eliminate all ancient superstitions, which have been unjustly attributed to religion, and religion could then shine forth in all its purity and glory. With mutual understanding between nations, humanity could receive vigorous international and interdenominational impulses. Soon there will be only two religions—the religion of love and the religion of ceremonial formalism.

The coming into power of Communism has meant prison, torture and death for thousands of Christians, but it has helped our thinking enormously: Communists think on a global plane, and in terms of future generations. The children of God, quite wrongly, have a reduced horizon: often their thinking is narrow, and they look only one step ahead. Was it for nothing that the leaders of the Church in the New Testament were called "presbyters", that is to say, people who see far ahead?

The Christian Jews, too, have learned to think on the universal plane, and to strive to achieve a distant goal. The Roman Empire threw Christians to the wild beasts, but it also taught them to think on an imperial scale. Christianity became the religion of the empire, instead of that of isolated individuals. Communism has played the same role for us.

The earth has plants which are used to heal individuals. The Bible tells us that Heavenly Jerusalem has leaves which serve to heal whole nations (Rev. 22.2). Christian Jews know the secret of finding their pharmaceutical remedies here.

Yet the evangelisation of the individual still remains the priority. Only saints can sanctify society. A social gospel preached to unregenerate men is a fake. But men who have been born again must bring their new life into society.

Christian revolutionism

We Christians were not frightened by Communist revolutionism. After all, we ourselves are the descendants of a revolutionary movement. Four hundred years ago, Calvin, in his commentary on the Book of Daniel, wrote: "The princes of this world set aside all their power when they rise against God, and are not worthy to be reckoned among mankind. We should rather spit in their faces than obey them when they are so bold as to try to deprive God of His rights . . . If they rise against God, they must be humbled and regarded as valueless as a pair of worn shoes." Before him, St. John Chrysostom and St. Ambrose had valiantly opposed emperors.

We do not reproach the Communists for their revolutionism, but for the fact that it has not gone far enough.

The Bible is much more revolutionary than the writings of Karl Marx and Lenin. On the very first page of the Bible we read that God says to the human beings He has just created: "Have dominion over the fish of the sea, and over the fowl of the air, and over every living thing that moveth upon the earth" (Gen. 1.28). Only notice this! Man is to have dominion over all nature, but not over another human being.

The Bible also tells us that God created only one couple: the English rebels at the time of the Peasants' Revolt understood this excellently when in one of their revolutionary songs they asked: "When Adam delved and Eve span, who was then the gentleman?"

God has made "all nations of one blood", the Bible declares (Acts 17.26), thus putting under a question mark the value of all titles of nobility and rank—including those in Socialist countries, such as Party membership or working-class origins— and all racialist theories.

The first nationalisation of landed property which aimed at preventing the exploitation of the peasants by the rich landowners in times of famine was put into practice by Joseph, when he was prime minister of Egypt.

In the preamble to the Ten Commandments, God boasts not of creating Heaven and Earth, but of something quite different: "I am the Lord thy God, which have brought thee out of the land of Egypt, out of the house of bondage." (Ex. 20.2) We are permitted no other gods apart from the God who makes it His task to liberate mankind from every sort of serfdom.

What a revolution the world underwent when the Sabbath was introduced as an institution! In pagan countries slaves were part of the machinery of production; the Bible introduced the principle that a man should rest, and that his servant should be given an opportunity to do likewise. In the Socialist countries, where the fulfilment of the various state plans is more important than Sunday rest, the fourth commandment, to keep the Sabbath, is a revolutionary imperative.

"Thou shalt neither vex a stranger, nor oppress him" (Ex. 22.21) is what the Bible teaches men in an age when being black in America and white in Africa and a Jew in Europe involves discrimination.

God commanded Moses not to treat the poor unjustly (Lev. 19.15). If the capitalist countries would respect this principle everywhere, they would have no need to fear the Communist threat.

We must remember that the sacred book of the apostles and the first Christians was the Old Testament, and not the New Testament, which was not written until several decades later. If Jesus had not intended to give His disciples a revolutionary training, what point was there in letting them read a book which was mainly an epic of revolutionary struggle?

The Lord raised up a deliverer for the children of Israel, the Benjamite Ehud, the man who killed the tyrant Eglon (Judges 3). Jael was called "blessed above women" for slaying the oppressor Sisera by driving a tent peg through his temple (Judges 5.24); these were the very words that were later on used about the mother of our Lord. Jael was what today would be called a brave female partisan in the army of liberation in an oppressed country. Other biblical characters, such as Gideon and Jephthah, were also revolutionary champions.

The Bible ridicules absolute monarchy in Jotham's parable which compares tyrants with thorn bushes while the useful trees, such as the olive, the fig and the vine, refused to play this odious role. In his speech when the Jews wished to elect a king, the prophet Samuel also inveighed against absolute monarchy. In the second book of Kings we read of the bloody revolution raised by Jehu against the tyranny of the Ahab dynasty. The Bible tells us that this revolution was carried out on the express orders of God. Jehu slew the two unlawful kings, and Queen Jezebel was thrown out of the window. He destroyed those who supported the tyranny and the sons of tyrants, and slew without mercy all priests who had made power an excuse for plunder. Not one was allowed to escape. After all this, the Lord said to Jehu: "Thou hast done well in executing that which is right in mine eyes, and hast done unto the house of Ahab according to all that was in mine heart" (2 Kings 10.30).

Later on, Jesus was to say: "Not everyone that saith unto me, 'Lord, Lord,' shall enter into the kingdom of heaven; but he that doeth the will of my Father which is in heaven" (Matt. 7.21). And the will of God, according to the book of Kings, in the story of the revolutionary Jehu, is the complete destruction of tyranny.

What revolutionary songs there are in the Bible! What is the *International* compared to Psalm 109, which is directed against the man who "persecuted the poor and needy man, that he might even slay the broken in heart"?

The cry for social justice echoed by the prophets of Israel is well known; in the New Testament, too, there are numerous revolutionary passages. The mother of our Lord establishes a social programme for her Son, whom she had conceived by the Holy Ghost, with the words: "He hath put down the mighty from their seats, and exalted them of low degree. He hath filled the hungry with good things; the rich he hath sent empty away" (Luke 1.52–53).

"Woe unto you that are rich!" said Jesus, "for ye have received your consolation! Woe unto you that are full! for ye shall hunger" (Luke 6.24–25). "It is easier for a camel to go through the eye of a needle, than for a rich man to enter into the kingdom of God" (Matt. 19.24).

"If a man does not work, he shall not eat," the fundamental principle in the legislation of Socialist states, is copied, almost word for word, from the Apostle Paul (2 Thess. 3.10).

Christians know that God has a chosen people, the Jews, and a chosen group, the Church, but how many know that He has a chosen social class? The apostle James wrote about something that was very familiar to his readers at that time: "Hath not God chosen the poor of this world?" (Jas. 2.5), and scourges the rich unmercifully.

"Christianity was formed as a religion for the poor, for

those who were exploited and oppressed, for the slaves and freed bondmen," writes Amusin, the Soviet historian, in his book on the Dead Sea Scrolls.

Within the Christian community there have always been those who have striven to return to the original teaching; but most have become hypnotised by details, controversies about baptism, speaking in tongues, and keeping the Sabbath, which might have been practised by the early Church but are not the essentials. But why should we not return to the revolutionism of the first Church, and the struggle to live according to the principles of social justice? When God chose a language in which to express His revelations in the Bible, He chose the Hebrew language, possibly the only language in which the verb "to have" does not exist. In this way He wished to show that the idea of property, of owning anything, is and must be completely alien to the people of God. It will always be true, as Jesus said, that the believer who wishes to attain perfection must "sell everything he has", and "leave all he has", and "leave home and family".

Proudhon's saying that "Property is theft" is one to which every believing Christian can subscribe; because as God has arranged things we are not meant to have property. All good things must be enjoyed in fellowship; individual ownership is an abomination. Only individual stewardship is admissible. Though private property is economically the best method of increasing riches, these should then be spent not for a selfish end, but for the glory of God and the good of one's fellow-men.

The Catholic Church, which faithfully recommends this teaching of Jesus, adopts the selfsame ideology today, even though it does not practise it. It declares that the man who wishes to be perfect must renounce private ownership, and only possess things in common, for example within the framework of a monastic order.

Today, at the threshold of a new historical era, Jews who believe in Jesus and faithfully follow His teaching are wholeheartedly on the side of the exploited and the oppressed. But we know of nobody more oppressed and more exploited than the citizens of the Socialist states, which speak in the name of the poor.

We utterly oppose Communist dictatorship and terror. We abhor Communist atheism. But, as a Christian must be "a Jew to the Jews and a Greek to the Greeks", so, in dealing with Communists, in the same sense we must be Communists, if we wish to win them for Christ. It is just as impossible to win them if we adopt an anti-Communist approach as it would be impossible to win Jews by adopting anti-Semitism. Though we are opposed to Communism, we must show sympathy for the individual Communist, just as St. Paul, who detested Greek idolatry, would use words of praise for the Greeks in order to convert them.

The writings of Socialism always offered us a great many Christian arguments. Whenever I meet a Communist who makes fun of the Bible as a reactionary book, I counter him with a quotation from Marx: "When Luther translated the Bible, he placed in the people's hands a powerful weapon against princes, nobility and clergy."

Whenever a Communist calls the Bible absurd, I quote from Engels' work *Bruno Bauer and Primitive Christianity:* "A religion which conquered the Roman world empire, and which has reigned for eighteen hundred years over the majority of civilised mankind, cannot be rejected merely by declaring that it consists of a series of absurdities, created by deceivers." In *The Revelation* he praises primitive Christianity as "a great revolutionary movement". It was, incidentally, Engels who wrote: "We live in God. One can understand that better when one travels on the sea."

Even the apostles took it for granted that the multitude would have to go away from Jesus to look for food; but Jesus showed that they could have food in plenty if they remained with Him.

No one need abandon Jesus in order to be a revolutionary. He can be a much better revolutionary by remaining with Him. Without Jesus, revolutions are destructive, and costly in blood. A revolution with Jesus is constructive, changing social conditions peacefully, after sanctifying hearts.

We were always present at the great Communist rallies, where we handed out our tracts. These started with the subjects I have just outlined, and thanks to them we made contact with the Communist soul, and preached the crucified Christ.

Conflict with Communism

Yet we had no illusions; we knew that our differences with the Communists were fundamental.

They are totalitarians; they do not permit the slightest deviation from the line pursued by the Party. Why should they allow us, who are just as totalitarian, and want all people to belong completely to God, to go free?

By practising the methods used by Jesus and His apostles we were able to win some Communists for Christ, but this resulted in increased opposition towards us by the Party. They did not want understanding, loyalty and love, they merely wanted us to identify ourselves with their plans, and to be transformed into willing tools. But our love for them would not allow us to be opportunists, to flatter them, or to be their willing slaves. Out of love towards them, we had to show them their crimes. They avoided us because we posed the problem of sin, and the madness of the Cross as the only way to solve this problem.

There are sins which are caused by social conditions, and which can be removed on the social plane, as were the sins of slavery and polygamy. But there is a limit to this. Lenin writes: "We can abolish the law that allows the capitalist to exploit the worker and the landowner to exploit the peasant, but no one in the world can prevent the cunning man exploiting the simple person, or the weak being exploited by the strong."

Communists, in the first case, would attain the limit of what is humanly possible by changing social conditions, but they cannot change human hearts. This only Jesus can do. He can give us new birth. Without using coercion, he turned cunning men like Matthew and Zacchaeus, and a terrorist like Saul of Tarsus, into good, just people. It is only the Cross of Jesus that can perform this miracle.

With Communists, as with all other people, the attempt to lead a moral life and to allow the mind to soar upwards is frustrated by sin which weighs down the soul with its enormous burden. They have committed injustices, they have made men weep, they have shed blood, they have been inconsistent and unfaithful to their own ideals, they have violated their own moral standards. This gives them a feeling of guilt, and of the need to be saved, but the more these are suppressed, the more they upset their mental state, resulting in all kinds of morbid and evil complexes.

And Communists do just what all other people do: they try to transfer their guilt to others, they look for a scapegoat. Adam blamed Eve, and Eve blamed the serpent. The Communists find their scapegoat in the bourgeoisie, the landowners, the Social Democrats, the Trotskyites, the clergy, the sectarians and their own Party members. They fight against everyone and everything.

No one can live in a constant mental attitude of "I am not worthy". Besides, the feeling of guilt is deaf to all argument. It is no good blaming our sins on bad heredity, or physical weakness; nor can we blame a bad social environment. Nor is it possible to blame Satan for our sin, as that would be admitting that we had listened to him. No madness can be healed by argument, certainly not the madness induced by guilt. There are mad people who believe that they have a watch ticking in their head. It is impossible to convince them that it is not so. In cases of this kind doctors anaesthetise the patient, make a small incision in his cranium, bandage him and, when he wakes up, show him parts of a watch stained with blood which, they tell him, have been extracted from his head. This is precisely the case with the madness of an evil conscience. The innermost heart cannot be persuaded that a sin is the result of atavistic or social causes. We feel responsible for our own evil doings. For this there is only one remedy, which is another form of madness—the madness of the Cross. "Yes, you are guilty, you are full of guilt, you are the only guilty person," the great healer Jesus tells us. "You need a scapegoat. You must transfer your sin to another. Do not attempt to transfer it to an equal, because your equal will throw it back to you, heavier than it ever was. Transfer it to me! I represent the Creator. Like Him, I bear responsibility for the whole of Creation and everything that is done in it. It is right that I should take your sin upon myself. I have expiated your sin on the Cross." The liberating effect of this sacrificial atonement of Jesus on the soul which trusts in Him is tremendous.

But there are sick people whose sickness has become the very substance of their lives. The blind who live by begging are horrified at the thought of being healed, as this will compel them to work. Jesus's healing Cross causes the same sort of panic. The Communists are in this plight; for them sin, especially hatred, has become the core and substance of life. What would they do without it? We preached a crucified Lord, and we knew that we would be hated.

Communists are atheists; we were committed to God. The conflict was unavoidable. We knew that many thousands of Christians had suffered in the Soviet Union. We prepared ourselves for the same fate.

There was another point of conflict. After the war, the great question was as to which city was to become the capital of the United World of the future—Moscow or Washington? The world divided into two camps, the revolutionary and the anti-revolutionary, and two blocs were formed. We openly declared our conviction that the efforts of Moscow and Washington would be equally in vain as the capital of the future united world, under the aegis of Jesus, would be Jerusalem, which He called the city of the great king. "Out of Zion shall go forth the law, and the word of the Lord from Jerusalem," says the prophet Isaiah (2.3).

Some believe that salvation will come from Communism; others believe it will come from American democracy. We believe what Jesus says: "Salvation is of the Jews" (John 4.22), and the Jews will fulfil their role of salvation when they turn again to Jesus.

Noah prophesied that Japheth (from whom the Indo-European race is descended) "shall dwell in the tents of

Shem" (from whom the Jews are descended). In other words, the Indo-European race will live in the temporary social systems created by the Jews, according to the words uttered by the prophet thousands of years ago (Gen. 9.27). And Moses told Israel at a later date: "Thou shalt build a house, and thou shalt not live therein . . . Thou shalt plant vineyards . . . but shalt neither drink of the wine, nor gather the grapes" (Deut. 28.30, 39).

Let us see how these remarkable prophecies have been fulfilled!

The House of Christianity was built by Shem, by the Jews. In primitive Christianity, everything was derived from the Jews. It was from the Jews that "Christ came as concerning the flesh, who is over all God, blessed for ever," wrote the apostle Paul (Rom. 9.5). The Bible is Jewish. Luther denied the validity of the ecumenical councils, using as his argument the fact that they were not constituted by Jews. "God's word was entrusted only to them," he said. The apostles were Jews. The psalms which are sung in the churches were written by David. For many centuries the whole of Europe has lived in the tent of Shem. The dominant influence exercised by the Christian civilisation embraces the entire world in its sphere. Only the Jews remain outside the dwelling which they themselves erected. All races have rejoiced at the good grapes which the vine of Jesus has borne; the Jews alone have not tasted them.

The Renaissance, the flow of gold from the New World, and conflict within the Church shook the House of Christianity in the fifteenth and sixteenth centuries. It was then that Israel, in great haste, constructed a new house, the house of capitalism. In his book *Jewry and Capitalism*, Werner Sombart described the decisive role the Jews have played and still play in the creation of capitalism. Japheth's descendants, the Indo-Europeans, have all entered into this new "tent of Shem" in the sphere of influence of capitalism.

When capitalism had triumphantly established itself, a Jew, Karl Marx, declared war on it. The Jews have benefited from capitalism, but Judaism finds no peace in it. Countless young Jews have started on a crusade to create a new system, Communism. The role played by Jews in building this new house, in which Japheth was to live, is well known. Lenin's mother was a Jewess named Braun. This is recorded by Trotsky, who adds that Stalin forbade all mention of her origins, in order not to hurt the anti-Semitic feelings of the Russians. A great number of the leaders of the Russian Revolution were Jews—Trotsky, Zinoviev, Kamenev and others. In Hungary, Communism was led by Bela Kun and Tibor Szamuely, and later by Rakosi and Gero. In Rumania, too, the Jews played an important role when Communism was introduced. A number of people from all races dwell in this new Socialist system, in the building of which Jews have played such an important role, though not an exclusive one. Many of the officers of the Communist Secret Police were Jews, but not as many as the anti-Semites like to assert. There were plenty of full-blood Rumanians who tortured their co-nationals. But the Jews are also the most active against the Soviet government. They have again built a house in which they cannot live. Russia's anti-Communist freedom-fighters Daniel, Litvinov, the priests Eshliman and Jakunin, Knasnov-Levitin are Jews. Having contributed in such large measure to the erection of the Communist regime in Rumania, a great number of the Jews then left the country to settle in Israel.

The Jews have always been God's chosen People, entrusted with the task of carrying out His plans in history, in creating social regimes which, step by step, would prepare the material, cultural and intellectual conditions for God's kingdom on earth.

Now they have been entrusted with a new role. Once they have returned, as a nation, to Jesus, their king, they will have a decisive role in building a fourth house, the Kingdom of God, where the Wandering Jew will at last find rest. This kingdom, with its centre in Jerusalem, will constitute a rejection of capitalism as well as of Communism, or it might even embody the useful features of all past social systems.

The anti-Semites pay the Jews a great compliment when they insist that this nation, numerically so insignificant, exercises so much influence all over the world, and is the root of all evil.

At one time the Niagara Falls were a nuisance to the United States and Canada, because they laid waste thousands of acres of fruitful soil. Wise men, however, realised that if Niagara was capable of wreaking such great destruction, then it should be capable of doing a great deal of good, once it was harnessed and made to drive turbines and similar devices. Today, these great falls are an important source of electric power to both countries. The Jews do a great deal of evil, contend the anti-Semites. This means that they are a source of energy, and that they are also capable of doing a great deal of good. But if they are to do this, they must be united with the source of all good, Christ. Hence the tremendous importance of the Christian Mission to the Jews. Up till now, a mission of this kind has seemed utopian; but we have now reached a new phase in history, when the Jews are coming into their own.

Our working methods brought us into conflict with the Communist authorities. In 1948, they put me in prison.

EPILOGUE

When i was released from prison, my enemies in the Church, those who had collaborated with the Communists, declared that I was a heretic. This aroused people's curiosity, and a great many people were anxious to hear me preach and to read my books. The doors of the old Lutheran churches were opened to me, and I preached from a pulpit where no Jew had ever stood. Nor had a Jew at any time preached in the Greek Orthodox cathedrals and other places to which I was now invited. The vast majority of those who came to hear me were non-Jews. But for anyone who has dedicated himself to preaching the gospel to the Jews, it is most important to win non-Jews for Christ, since every person, no matter what his race, who has been converted to Jesus by a Jew, becomes himself a missionary to the Jews. This indirect approach is every bit as important as the direct approach.

As their latest attack had proved fruitless, my enemies now adopted different tactics, spreading the rumour that I was mad. But they spoke of my madness without any signs of sympathy, thus rendering their motives suspect from the very start.

I had long been used to hearing all sorts of things said about me. I had been called a genius, an idiot; "Jesus Christ", "the Devil"; a highly cultured person, an ignoramus; a saint, a repulsive character; a man of exemplary honesty, a thief; a Nazi, a Communist, an anarchist, a Jesuit; the most lovable and the most despicable accusation was that they now said I was mad. In believing that they were undermining the value of my message by calling me insane, my enemies revealed their own ignorance.

In the first place, there is a certain affinity between insanity and genius. Seneca wrote: "There is no great intellect that does not possess a touch of madness."

The Christian Jews had set themselves the task of building a road to Judaism and mankind. How could they carry out this task without a touch of madness? Some people reproached me for my madness but I asked, in the words of Nietzsche: "Where is the madness that you should be inoculated with?"

Christian Jews have a great vocation: they are expected to be grand, to attain to the stature of Christ, to do greater things than He did (John 14.12), to conquer the fortress of Israel, which He failed to conquer. If they attain to this greatness, they will also share the fate of all great men, one of whose characteristics is madness. In the prophetic Psalm 69 we hear of the madness of the Messiah. Paul confessed himself to be a fool. Without a touch of madness he would not have been a great apostle. Nervous disorders are commoner among people with a special vocation than among ordinary people. We were not in the least surprised when a young engineer, one of the most brilliant of our brethren, suddenly had a serious nervous breakdown, and had to go to hospital. This in no way lessened the value of his convictions.

The prejudice is widely held that a sound mind is valuable not only biologically but also socially. But history has not been moulded by normal people. Could Calvin and Luther have introduced the Reformation if they had been normal? Our object is to bring about a revolution within Christianity, within Judaism and in the world. Woe to the man with a vocation of this kind who is afraid of madness!

One of my enemies once said to me: "In Christianity everything must start from the beginning." When I answered: "Let us begin," he withdrew in fear, and to my great delight called me mad. When madness has reached a particular stage, it makes the intellect more sensitive, sharpening it and making it more perceptive to contrasts. This makes the mind more complicated, richer, more conscious of itself. Not for nothing did Erasmus of Rotterdam write his book *In Praise of Foolishness*. I thanked God that I had spent many years in prison in conditions which might well induce madness. My intellect had in many ways acquired new qualities, which I now used in serving Christ.

Besides, madness is close to love. Normal people bicker with their husbands or wives, and in some way or another have to put up with them. Romeo and Juliet were a bit mad, and so were the mystics. I like to call things by their right names. It is no secret to those who have read the lives of the great mystics that the mystic life is to a large extent nourished by unsatisfied sexual desires. Blessed is the man who can sublimate this desire to the spiritual world! In this respect, too, the years I spent in prison were of great help to me.

I had a mystical experience which ordinary people, living a normal sexual life and an abnormal family life of conflict and family quarrels, could never have had, and could never have understood. They would merely have dismissed it as madness or a farce. But my experiences were of great value because a Christian-Jewish pastor, if he were to fulfil our tremendous task, had to have—like the living creatures of the Revelation—four heads: the head of a mystic, the head of a man capable of scientific thought, the head of a strategist capable of organising, and the head of a revolutionary.

How can a normal, modern clergyman, whose chief source of reading seems to be Dale Carnegie's *How to Win Friends and Influence People* rather than the evangelists' *The Art of Discovering a Meaning in Allowing Oneself to be Crucified*, sublimate the tragedy of life, be filled with pathos, and weave his way through the infinite realms of metaphysics?

I accepted the label "mad". Has not God made foolish the wisdom of the world? For Christ's sake I want to be a fool, and not a peaceful, vulgar, banal, run-of-the-mill member of society.

I can look back on twenty-five years of strife. I have received many blows, but I have also delivered my share. Christians must be the salt of the earth, and also the mustard. They must sting. The enemy must know that he is facing a soldier of Jesus who is well armed.

I have known unspeakable joy and deep sorrow. The one thing I have never done is to be bored. Along the path that Jesus has prepared for us there is life in abundance.

Thanks to the grace of God I have met brethren of many nations who have given themselves entirely to the God of Israel. I have read that God has equipped them in this way in order to make the Jews envious. I envied them, and tried to be, like them, a faithful champion of the cause of Jehovah and of His chosen Son, Jesus. In my former days I had been an eager servant of Satan; now I wished to serve God in the same way.

I did this in an age of great spiritual indifference. Men eat, drink, marry and build houses without knowing the prophecies and without realising what is happening in Israel and in the world—that mankind is approaching the end of time, and the clock now shows five minutes to twelve.

Mankind must either be converted, or be destroyed in a nuclear catastrophe. We are striving to convert the world. We wish to bring the Jewish people to Christ, because not till then will there be new life in the Church, and not till then will the Christians be as they were described at the beginning of the second century by the Athenian orator Aristides:

"The Christians know God and trust in Him. They forgive those who oppress them, and make them their friends. They are good to their enemies. Their wives keep marriage pure; their daughters are chaste. They love one another. They do not refuse to help widows. When they see a stranger, they receive him in their house, and rejoice at him as at a brother. If any among them is poor or in need, they fast for two or three days in order to satisfy his needs. They obey conscientiously the commandments their Messiah has given them. Every morning and every hour they praise God and thank Him for His goodness. They are the source of all that is beautiful in the world. They do not speak publicly of their good deeds, but take good care not to be observed by any man. They are in truth a new people, and there is something divine in them."

The negative characteristics of the Christian Jews of today do not discourage us. These are not the result either of their

Judaism or of their Christianity, but of the strong pressure which the world exerts on them. Circumstances will change when the whole of Israel is saved. But even today the Christian Jew, who in truth is a Jew and in truth a Christian, who does not claim to be a Rumanian or a German, a Lutheran or a Catholic, is a source of great blessing to the nation. Many Christians, ecclesiastical as well as lay, have adopted an entirely new attitude to Christianity, and it was the Christian Jews who gave them the first impulse in this direction.

As yet, however, we have only taken the first steps. Those who wish to follow us will have to work in an entirely different way. We have only been able to work by winning a soul here and a soul there. We shall have to think strategically, and work on a national front, in fact we shall have to think in terms of universal perspectives, since new factors have arisen.

Every day, the Devil takes tens of thousands of people with him to hell. We do not bruise the serpent's head, but only tickle its stomach a little, if we are content merely to save one out of all these tens of thousands.

We must change the religious attitude of our people, and of the whole world. This is undoubtedly a difficult task, but everything is possible with God and with those who believe.

Jesus is not the Saviour whom the Jews seek. He wishes to save us from sin. We would like to keep sin, because it provides us with pleasures, and we only wish to be saved from the catastrophic consequence of sin. We want Him to speak to us about our economic and political problems, and to save Israel from oppression by other people, and enable her to triumph over them. But He speaks to us of lilies, of birds, and of an eternal kingdom of justice and light for all people.

But neither God nor the universe is as we would like it to be. It is not reality that must change into what we want, but we who must adapt ourselves to reality. The true prayer is "Thy will be done," and not "Lord, let my will be done."

By accepting Christ as He is, and showing Him our confidence, even when we do not understand Him, Israel will fulfil its sacred vocation, for which it has been chosen. We must receive Christ; and together with Him we shall in love

embrace all His disciples, from all nations, with all their faults
and shortcomings. Even a flawed diamond is, after all, more
valuable than a perfect grain of sand.

Our Gentile brethren surrounded us at all times with their
love, and without their help our missionary work among the
Jews would not have been possible.

When the Jews hunger after God, they will no longer take
offence at the fact that the Christians possess in an earthen
vessel the spiritual treasure they have received from Israel,
that they have sins. The Talmud declares: "The man who
blows on a glass of beer to remove the froth is not thirsty.
And if anyone asks: 'What shall I eat with my bread?' thou
shalt take the bread from him, because he is not hungry." We
too received spiritual sustenance from the testimony of the
weakest Christian.

What shall we do to conquer Israel?

In the first place we must not be dismayed at the magnitude
of our task. Jesus said: "Fear not, little flock; for it is your
Father's good pleasure to give you the kingdom" (Luke 12.32).

We shall not achieve our goal by analysing the enthusiasm
of our convictions, but by knowing Him in whom we believe,
and whom we preach: God.

To what does Israel owe its miraculous history? Could it
be to efficient propaganda? No, but to the fact that without
anyone else knowing about it, one of our forefathers overcame
an angel as he wrestled with him, and wrung from him an
eternal blessing.

Step by step the discovery by one man of a new source of
energy—steam, electricity, the atom—has changed the face of
the world. An unknown source of power still exists: the power
which we inherit from the good angels, and from the prophets
and the saints, who have departed this life without having
their longing fulfilled or witnessing what we are witnessing
today—the time when Jesus will come again. This power is
still latent today, and it can become effective. In one night an
angel slew 180,000 Assyrians. Having an angel on your side
is more valuable than having the support of crowds of big and
important people.

In order to unite Christian Jews with angels I spent years in prison, isolated from the brethren. This road is full of secrets, but it is the road along which we must walk. When the time comes we shall be clad in surpassing majesty, and Israel will belong to Christ.

When will this happen? It depends on how quickly each one of us starts out on this road.

What is demanded is that each of us should dedicate our life to the truth that is in Christ, and then the miracle will take place.

But here are two practical pieces of advice: first, concentrate your missionary efforts on the key personalities among the Jewish people; second, include in the missionary programme of your church the one third of Jewry which lives in the Communist world and which is subjected to heavy persecution.

What would you think of somebody who pays a pastoral visit to a family where one member is deadly sick and converses with the healthy ones without even inquiring about the one who is in bed? Two thirds of the Jews live in the free world or in their own country where, though facing troubles, they enjoy independence. How can a mission to the Jews not give priority to the problem of the Jews in the Soviet Union who are terrorised, kept apart for mockery and blows, but not allowed to cultivate their specific Jewish values, language, art and religion?

How will it end? There is not much chance that they will be allowed to go to Israel. Even if allowed, how could Israel take in a short time over three million new inhabitants? And how will they rejudaize three million men and women who certainly hate Communism, but have been indoctrinated only with Marxism? They know no other teaching than that of fierce atheism, wherewith they have been brainwashed. For the time being in any case, these Jews are in the U.S.S.R. and they are there to stay.

Any sensible man will tell you that there is not the slightest possibility of convincing them to become Orthodox Jews. Who will spread this religion to them? There exists no Orthodox mission even to the Jews in the free world. For a missionary work in conditions of illegality Orthodox Judaism is completely unprepared. Neither would such a mission have the slightest probability of succeeding. Should liberal Judaism try the adventure? What will it propagate? The doubts of modernism? The criticism of the Bible? The religious problem will come to the forefront again, and in the spirit I already see Jewish synagogues, schools, newspapers and publishing houses, Jews in all the key positions in political, economic, cultural, scientific and artistic life, in every country in the world, rallying to the service of Christ. I see people of all colours and races turning to the Jews, so that these can show them the way to the Saviour (Zech. 8.23). I see Jerusalem as the capital of the Christian world. I see peace, love, justice and understanding triumphing. I see the lion lie down with the lamb. I see a kingdom to which Jesus has returned to rule. I see an earthly life which is consciously used as a preparatory stage for eternal life. I see Jews in Christian pulpits, showing the peoples of the world the perfect way to salvation. Faith sees all these things, and this is how it will be. For I do not believe the reality before my eyes, but the promises of God.

The dawn is appearing; soon it will be day; soon the sun will shine on Israel.

This was the hope that inspired Nollensen, the Batakians' apostle from Sumatra, and with his own eyes he saw the fulfilment of his dream. It was the hope of Skrefsrud for the Santalis, of Paton for the New Hebrides, and many others.

The Jews live on an entirely different level, and it is much more difficult to convert them. They are a race which has a great many outstanding personalities. But where God is there to help us, there is no difference between what is difficult and what is easy.

Up to the present the majority of the Jews have not believed in Jesus, not because they wanted it so, but because God has concealed the truth from them (Matt. 11.25). And God has remained hidden from them, because He wished to retain them as His strategic reserve. They are the future hope of the Church. God has spared them from fifteen centuries of error and decline in the Church, because this would enable Him to use the Jews, who were not tainted with these sins, to re-establish the Church at the decisive moment.

That moment has come; and now Christ will be King of the Jews.

*Inquiries and gifts for preaching the Gospel among
the Jews of Communist countries
should be addressed to:*

Christian Mission to the Communist World
Jewish Department
P.O. Box 19
Bromley
Kent, BR1 1DJ
England